SECRET FROME

Andrew Pickering & Gary Kearley

AMBERLEY

To Lisa and Sue

First published 2019

Amberley Publishing
The Hill, Stroud
Gloucestershire, GL5 4EP

www.amberley-books.com

ISBN 978 1 4456 7266 3 (print)
ISBN 978 1 4456 7267 0 (ebook)

British Library Cataloguing in Publication Data.
A catalogue record for this book is available from the British Library.

Origination by Amberley Publishing.
Printed in Great Britain.

Contents

Introduction

Frome, it is said, was founded in the late seventh century by followers of St Aldhelm, Abbot of Malmesbury. Aldhelm and his monks, so the story goes, founded a church dedicated to St John the Baptist and around it grew the settlement that eventually became the town. The older name for Frome – Frome Selwood – denotes its location in Selwood Forest, a royal forest that straddles the Somerset–Wiltshire border and extends south almost into Dorset. The forest was remembered in around 1800 as having been 'within the memory of man, the notorious asylum of a desperate clan of banditti, whose depredations were a terror to the surrounding parishes'. The poverty and disorder in certain parts were notorious. The prosperity and importance of Frome through the ages, nevertheless, is evident in its standing historic remains. By the 970s it had become a prosperous market centre, probably minting its own coins. It had a royal palace, and at least one Saxon king – Athelstan, in 934 – summoned his council there. Frome was the foremost of the ancient Frome Hundred parishes and liberties, the others being Beckington, Berkley, Cloford, East Cranmore, Elm, Laverton, Leigh on Mendip, Lullington, Marston Bigot, Mells, Nunney, Orchardleigh, Rodden, Rode, Standerwick, Wanstrow, Whatley, Witham Friary and Woolverton. These are the subjects of this book.

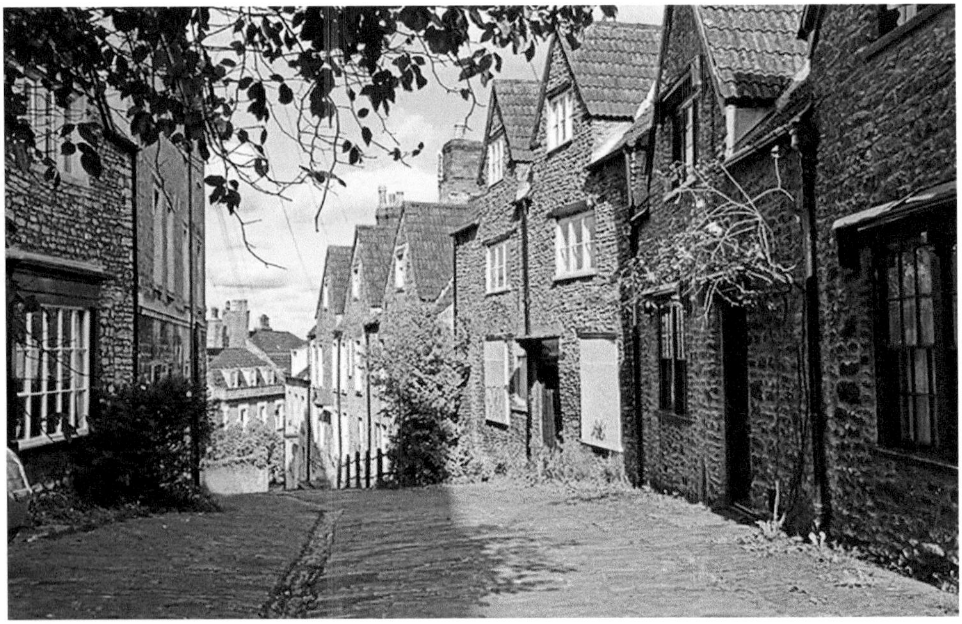

Gentle Street doubles as Truro in the TV adaptation of *Poldark*. (Robin Rowland Hill)

Frome's Anglo-Saxon heyday as a great ecclesiastical centre and resort of kings seems to have passed by the time of the Norman Conquest. Nevertheless, the town prospered as a busy commercial and woollen cloth manufacturing centre, noted by John Leland in the late 1530s for its fine stone houses. St John's Church was greatly altered in the late thirteenth century and the fortunes of Frome's clothiers contributed to further developments in the fifteenth century, before it was rebuilt again ('restored') in the nineteenth century.

The modern obsession with heritage and conservation has addressed, with considerable success, the age-old impulse to demolish, improve and rebuild; though much has been lost within living memory, much of 'old' Frome survives to tell the story of its past. Gentle Street in Frome has become familiar to millions of viewers as 'Truro' in the hugely popular recent BBC dramatisation of the *Poldark* stories.

As Frome's manufacturing base decayed in recent decades and long-established businesses closed their premises, the town has regenerated as an increasingly fashionable cultural hub. Frome has an enduring association with the arts and crafts that can be traced back at least as far as the founding of Singer's brassworks in the nineteenth century. If it was indeed 'sometimes dismissed as a fuddy-duddy place near Bristol', when Michael McGarvie was writing his history in the late 1970s, it is no more. Instead it is known for its progressive outlook, architectural charm, and a location in one of the most desirable parts of the country for those wishing to settle beyond city limits – the best in the South West according to a 2018 report in the *Sunday Times*. In recent years several

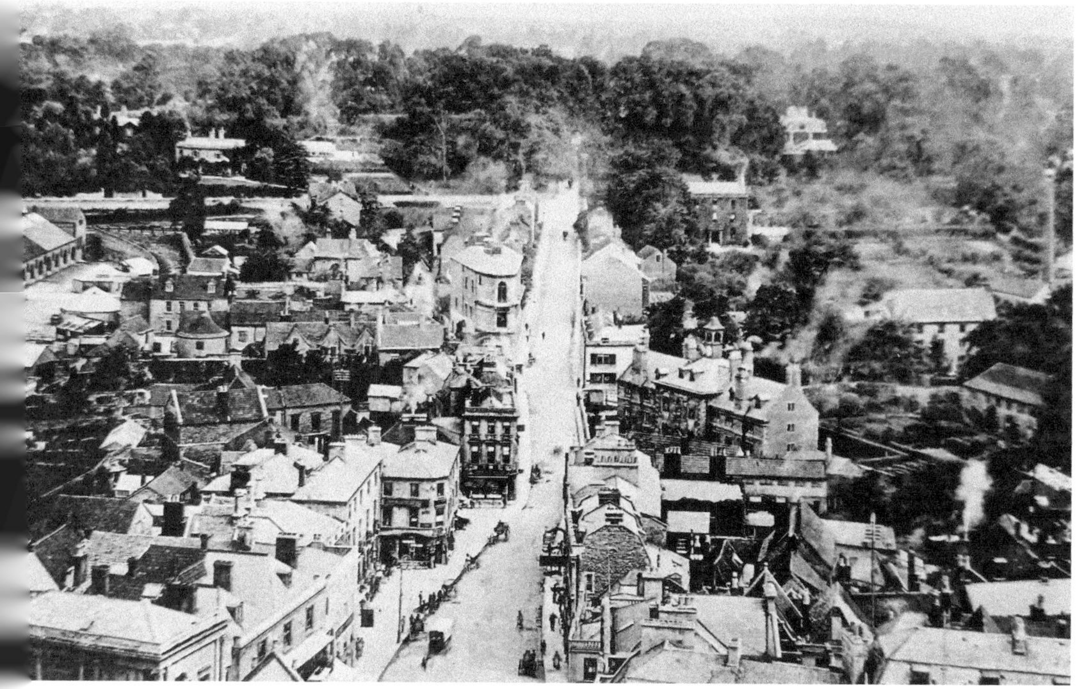

Frome Market Place, *c*. 1910.

ambitious not-for-profit community initiatives have been launched, a 'Frome Pound' alternative currency was introduced, the country's first state-funded Steiner school with its offer of an alternative to mainstream education opened, and the 'Independents for Frome' party secured every seat on the town council. The annual Frome Festival, running over several days in July, celebrates the arts to popular acclaim; independent shops thrive in the town centre; and bijou street markets celebrate diversity in taste and fashion. Wholefood cafés and artisan bistros have joined, and sometimes replaced, the host of more traditional food and drink outlets. The cosy teashop image of the town portrayed in the eighties, when maverick TV chef Keith Floyd visited The Settle, has given way to the hip-hop world of the Cheese and Grain, hosting gigs by numerous stars at the cutting edge of contemporary culture, and occasional unannounced ones by the likes of the Foo Fighters.

While the Frome Hundred edition of the Victoria County History, long awaited, is yet to be written, the general history of the town and its environs has been told elsewhere, and McGarvie's *Book of Frome* has been especially helpful in the compilation of this one, which attempts to shed light on the lesser-known aspects of the area's fascinating, and often surprising, history – a 'secret' history, perhaps, for many readers when they first turn its pages.

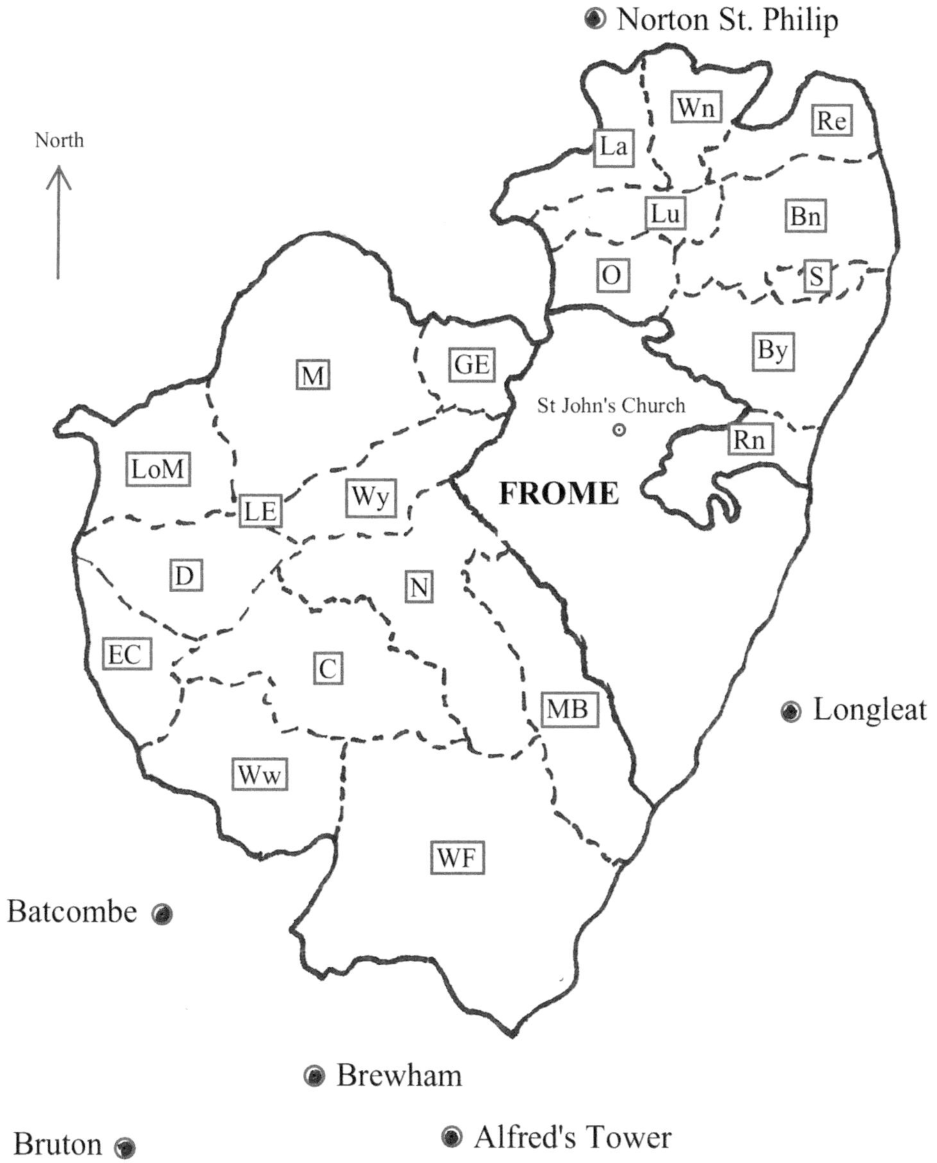

Frome and its hundreds.

Key.

Bn: Beckington	GE: Great Elm	M: Mells	Rn: Rodden
By: Berkley	La: Lavington	MB: Maiden Bradley	S: Standerwick
C: Cloford	LE: Little Elm	N: Nunney	Wn: Woolverton
D: Downhead	LoM: Leigh on Mendip	O: Orchardleigh	Ww: Wanstrow
EC: East Cranmore	Lu: Lullington	Re: Rode	Wy: Whatley

1. Underground Frome

Few who stand and admire Frome's elegant Georgian buildings, including the Grade I listed Rook Lane Chapel and The Blue House, realise that there is a whole different world under their feet, with structures that predate anything found above ground.

Driving or walking across the town bridge, one could easily be forgiven for thinking that it hasn't changed much over the years. Not so. There has been a stone bridge on this site for over 550 years, the original bridge being built in 1451 when increased traffic meant that the old ford taking the road across the river towards Bath was inadequate. A new wider bridge was built in 1667, but rather than destroy the old bridge, the new one was simply built alongside. Look underneath the bridge and you will discover that there are actually four bridges there, one beside the other as two further extensions were constructed. When North Parade was constructed in 1797, to provide a more auspicious entrance to the town from Bath, the bridge had to be slightly widened to align it to the new road. This realignment left the original part of the bridge that led onto the old approach road, Bridge Street, obsolete, and such was the rivalry with Bath at this time, that in 1821 it was decided to erect buildings on the unused part of the bridge to mimic Bath's famous Pulteney Bridge. It is said that the buildings on Frome's bridge, designed by George Underwood, were constructed to three and, in one case, four stories simply because Pulteney Bridge only had two-storey buildings. The erection of these buildings unduly restricted the width of the bridge, necessitating another small extension to enable the footpath to be retained. It is therefore true to say that when one crosses Frome Bridge one is actually crossing four bridges built in 1451, 1667, 1797 and 1821. The bridge remains one of only a handful in England that have buildings across their entire length.

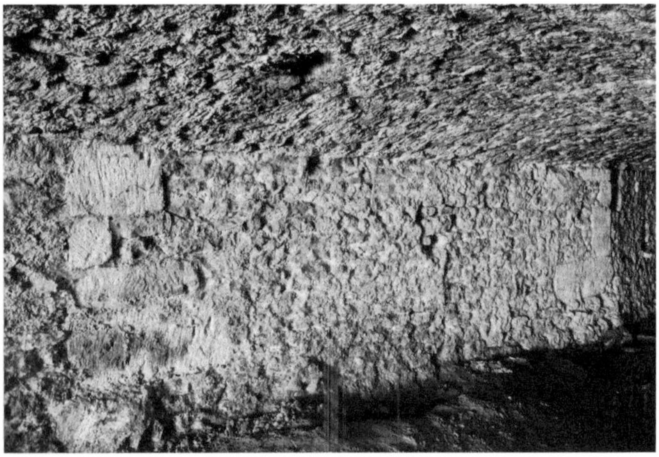

Anglo-Saxon building built into the foundations of Frome Bridge. (Martin Kearley)

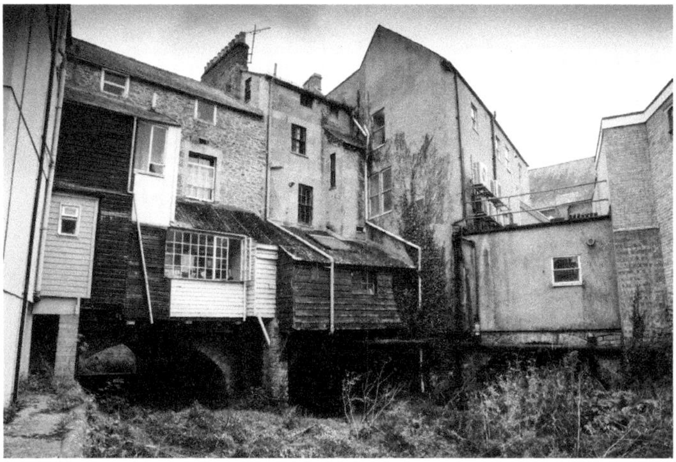

The lesser-known side of Frome Bridge. (Martin Kearley)

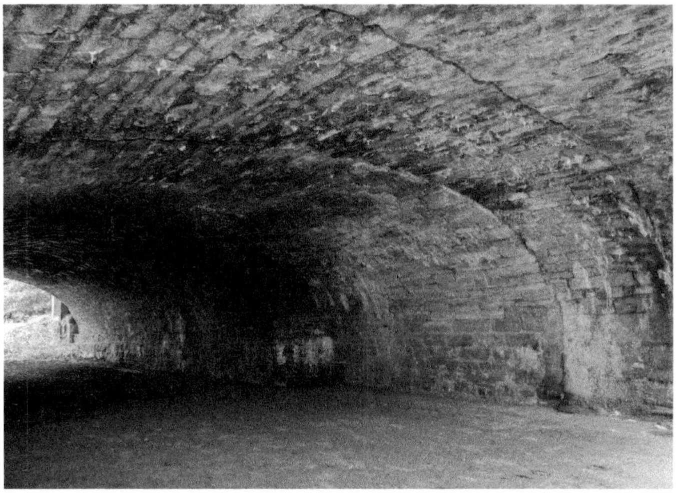

Four periods of construction visible under Frome Bridge. (Martin Kearley)

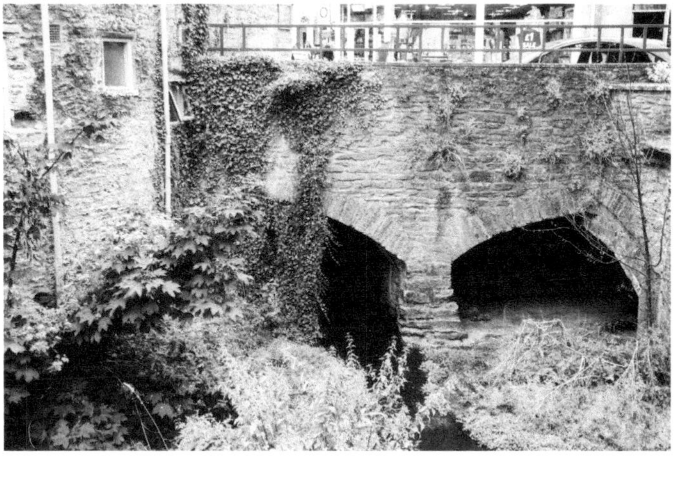

Some of the tunnels under Frome Bridge. (Martin Kearley)

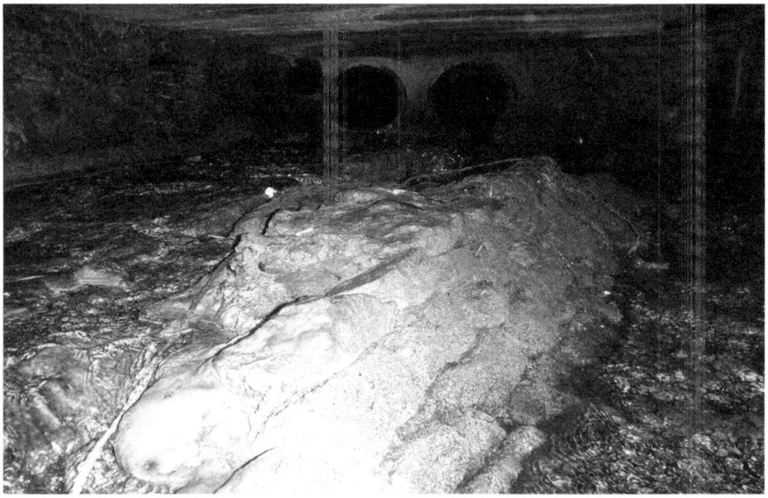

Medieval road beneath Frome Bridge. (Robin Rowland Hill)

Parts of the medieval road that led to the ford can still be seen, built into the foundations of the 1451 bridge. Also incorporated into the foundations are what are believed to be the remains of a stone-built Saxon guardhouse, constructed to protect the ford and, no doubt, to collect taxes and tolls from travellers. Most of this ancient roadway disappeared when the ground level in and around the market square was raised to provide more flood-free building land for the burgeoning town. In many places, the ground level was raised by the simple expedient of adding an extra storey to buildings, with the original street level rooms then effectively becoming cellars. Beneath the Wheatsheaves pub on Bath Street (since renamed No. 23 Bath Street) doorways and windows that faced onto the original road can be seen in what are now the cellar walls. This flood prevention work was not wholly successful, as evidenced by the severe flooding that frequently took place in this area, until the river was realigned in 1969.

There exists below Frome's streets a vast complex of tunnels, whose origins are now shrouded in mystery. Certainly, many of these structures were built as drains to take away the large volume of water emanating from the numerous springs to the south of the town. As the town grew, these previously open ditches were covered over to release more land for building, becoming tunnels in the process. Other tunnels, especially around Willow Vale, were deliberately constructed as flues for the drying towers and chimneys that served the once thriving wool dyeing business. It is hard to imagine that this quiet, pretty little street was once a noisy, smelly, smoky hive of industry. Other tunnels were built to carry water to drive industrial machinery, for example at the Silk Mill, and short stretches of these types of tunnels are still to be found under gardens or car parks throughout the town. However, the majority of Frome's tunnels do not fall into any of these categories and seem to have been constructed to allow for the passage of people, generally being 5 to 6 feet high and 3 to 4 feet wide. Indeed, older residents of Frome tell of playing in these tunnels as children, often using them to visit friends in other parts of the town without once having to come above ground. All the entrances to this system have now been blocked, either by safety-conscious local authorities or by

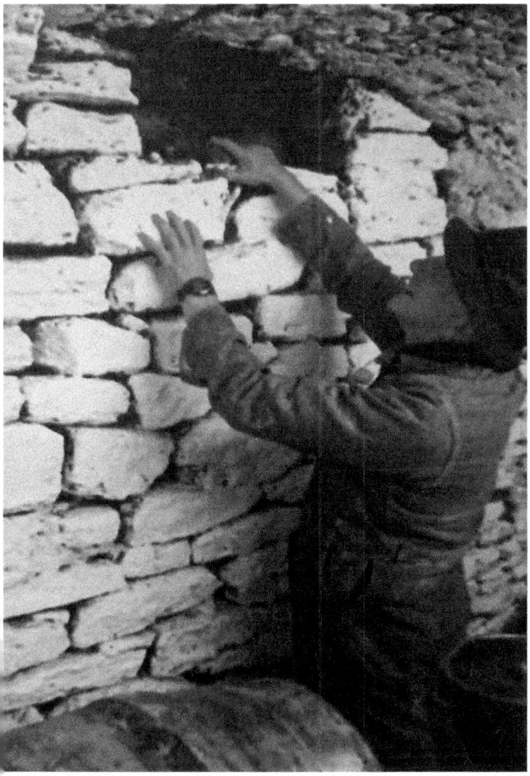

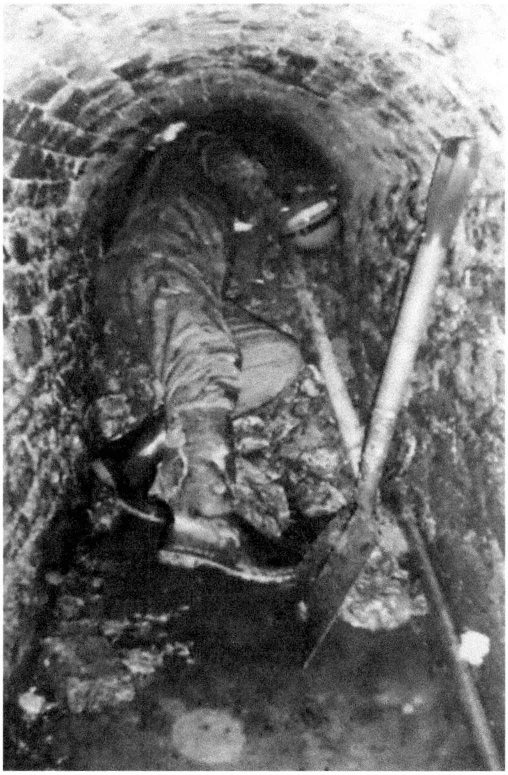

Above left: Under the Griffin pub in Milk Street. (Robin Rowland Hill)

Above right: Water tunnel under the Silk Mill, used to drive machinery. (Robin Rowland Hill)

security-minded property owners. In many places the blocked tunnel entrances are still clearly visible in cellar walls, especially in the older Trinity and Catherine Hill areas of the town. Members of the Frome Tunnels Project started to dismantle the wall blocking a tunnel under the Griffin public house, but this work had to stop and the stones replaced when it was realised that the top of the tunnel was very close to the road above. Evidently an unauthorised attempt was made to reopen the tunnel some time later and it came as no surprise when it was reported that a beer delivery lorry had fallen through the pavement outside the pub.

The questions remain: when were they built and why? A number of these tunnels are very short, often going from a property on one side of the road to a property on the other. There are known examples on North Parade and on Trinity Street where one Henry Baily was once landlord of both the Crown & Sceptre and the Bell Inn opposite. Until the late nineteenth century, brewing was very much a cottage industry, with many pubs producing their own beer, and one explanation for these short tunnels, such as the one between Baily's premises, is that they were built to allow the easy movement of beer from pubs that brewed their own to those that did not. It made sense to build a short tunnel under a road rather than having to haul heavy barrels in and out of cellars.

DID YOU KNOW?
'Selwood' is thought to derive from the Saxon word 'sealhwudu', meaning 'woodland where willow ('sallow') trees grow'. However, the term 'forest' derives from the Latin word '*foras*', meaning outside – originally it had no particular association with woodland. Royal forests, where special rules applied, were not absolutely subject to (were 'outside') the common law. The king's foresters were much resented for the special privileges that came with their appointment.

Longer tunnels also exist. The best known is the one that starts in a garden to the north of Willow Vale, which is said to go under the river and emerge near the churchyard of St John's. The location of the Willow Vale entrance was discovered by enthusiasts in 2012 following detailed descriptions from a man who lived there as a child. The exact location of the other end of the tunnel is unknown, although a story of its possible rediscovery by builders working on a house in Gentle Street in the 1980s came to light in 2017. After exploring the tunnel, the builders are said to have blocked it up again for fear of getting into trouble with the owner of the property. When the house was later sold the new owner tried to find out more but the builders could not remember exactly where the entrance was, their memories, apparently, shrouded by drinking too much at lunchtimes. All they could recall was that the tunnel ran parallel to the churchyard before turning sharply towards the river. Despite extensive investigations at the house no trace has yet been found of its elusive southern end.

No map exists of what might amount to a network of tunnels under the town, although local interest groups have made a start, drawing on anecdotes and by dowsing. To date only one historic record of one of Frome's tunnels has been found: the deeds of a property

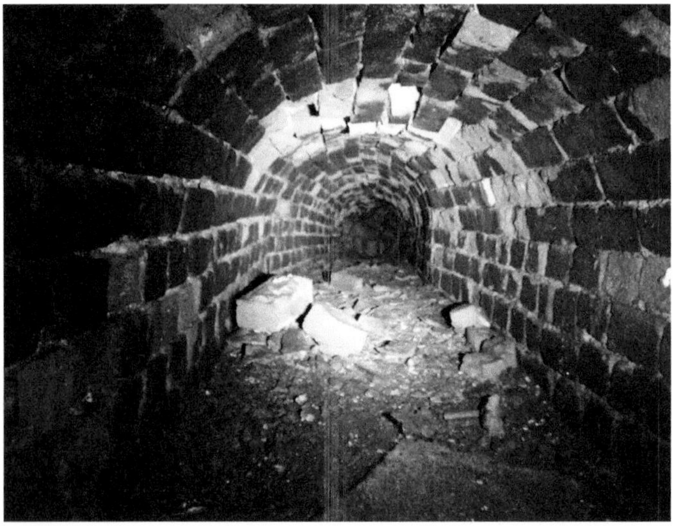

Flue under a garden in Willow Vale. (Robin Rowland Hill)

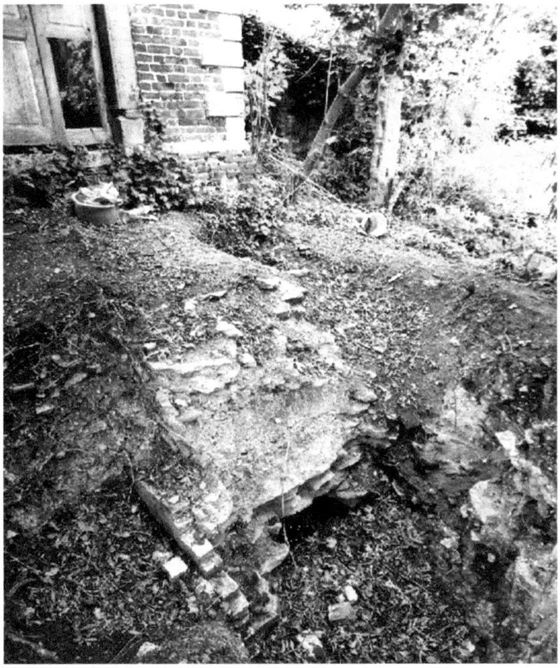

Partially uncovered tunnel entrance in Willow Vale (centre bottom). (Robin Rowland Hill)

in Eagle Lane show a dotted line running under Bath Street and into the Wheatsheaves pub. The pub's tunnel entrance was concealed when the lower cellars were abandoned and a new concrete floor was laid; the search for the Eagle Lane entrance continues. It is thought that this entrance could be somewhere in the cellars that house the town's electrical transformers, moved there during the Second World War to protect them from German bombs. Frome has a long tradition of weapon making and a number of factories in the town were involved in the production of military equipment. Evans Engineering's Adderwell Works made machine guns, Singer's produced munitions, and Notts in Merchant Barton fabricated Carley lifeboats. Frome was bombed by the Luftwaffe in 1941 so the move to protect the transformers was well justified.

While Frome is a long way from the sea, there might be a grain of truth in the romantic tradition that the tunnels served a role in the movement of smuggled goods, but the function of many of these tunnels remains conjectural. It is said that there are three large tunnels that come into Frome from Longleat House (7 km away), Nunney Castle (6 km) and Beckington Castle (5 km), all built as escape routes. The recollections of those who used them, mostly during or just after the Second World War, when their precise location was known and access was still possible, exist as first-hand accounts. Beckington Castle was used by Ravenscroft School from 1945 to 1970 and the English teacher would take the boys into the tunnels as a treat. Accessed through panels in the huge manorial fireplaces, former pupils remember sliding down within the depth of the walls to emerge in the tunnel. By this time the branch leading towards Standerwick had collapsed but the other tunnel continued towards Frome, passing under the Ship Inn (now Jay's Kitchen) where the boys recalled that the tunnel was so near to the road that the traffic could be heard overhead.

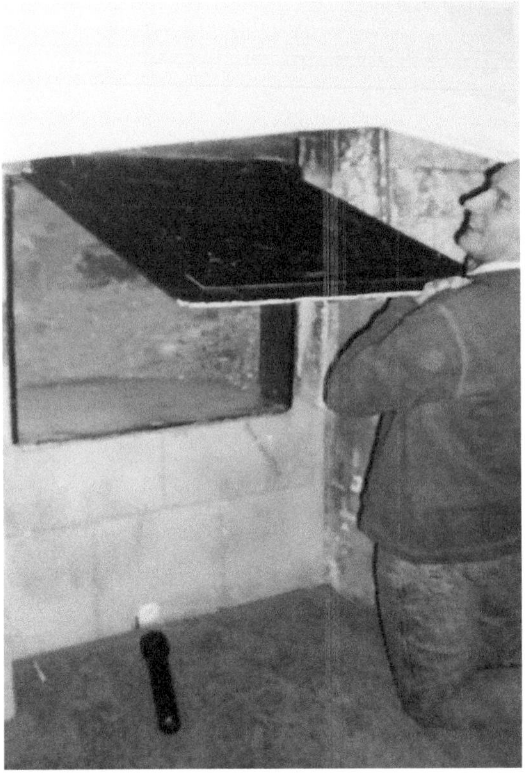

Left: Entrance to the tunnels under Beckington Castle. (Robin Rowland Hill)

Below: Two blocked-up entrances in a cellar on Trinity Street. (Robin Rowland Hill)

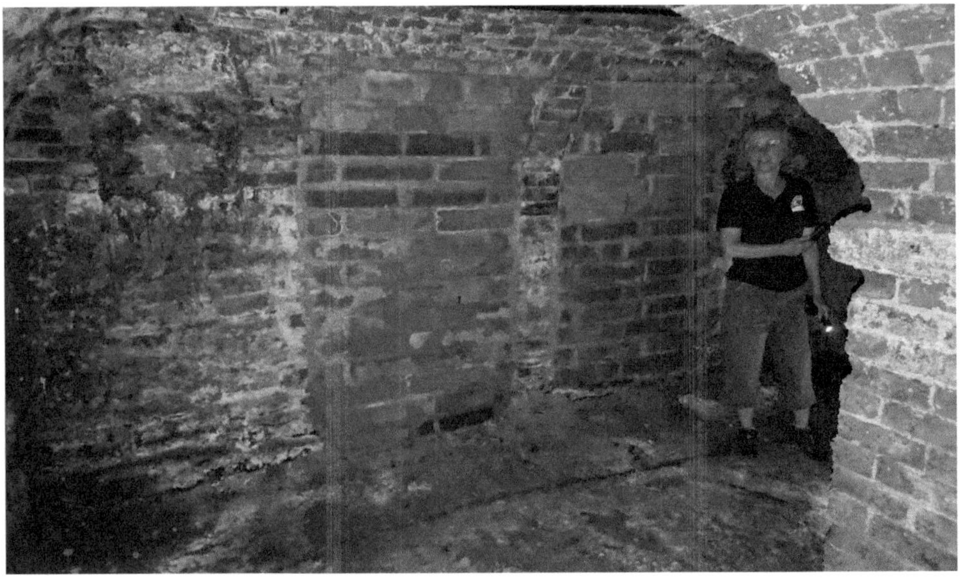

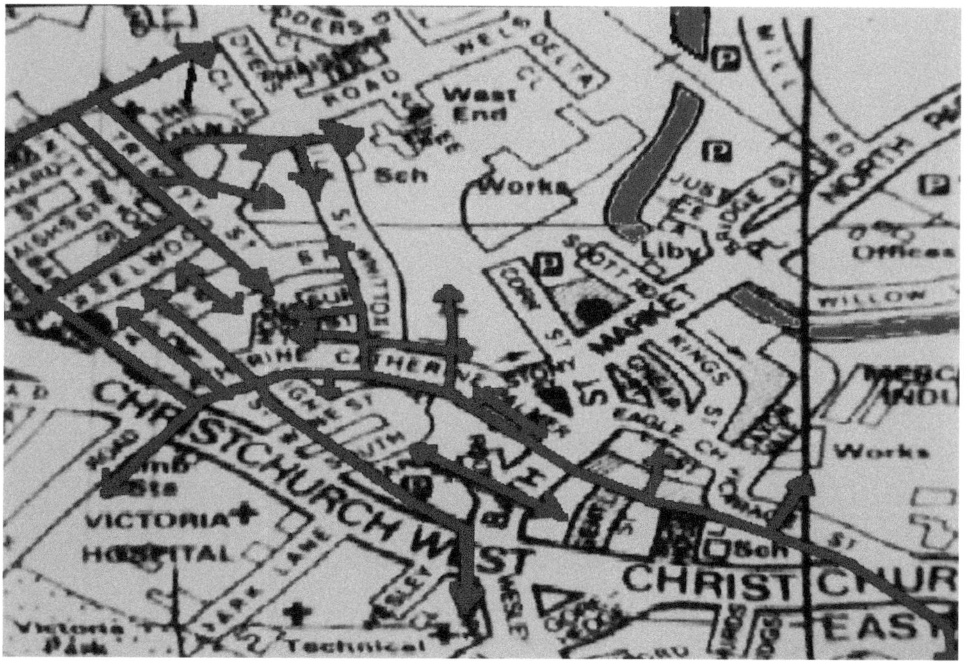

Map produced by dowser Don Reeves.

The tunnel from Nunney was accessed from a quarry behind the castle, now a car park. Witnesses recall that it was 'as tall as my father and just as wide' and was made of cut stone blocks the whole way. They say that it took them nearly two hours to walk to Frome, underground the whole way, emerging in the new foundations of Oakfield School on which building work had been suspended due to the Second World War. Longleat is said to have at least one other tunnel, which leads from the house to Heaven's Gate. The daughter of a former Longleat employee recalled how, in the immediate aftermath of the Second World War, her father turned up for work to find that the lake at the house had disappeared, having drained into a collapsed tunnel beneath it. The estate workers are said to have spent all weekend filling sandbags left over from the war and throwing them into the tunnel from the bridge. Once the work was completed the lake slowly refilled. This tunnel was plotted by dowser Don Reeves during filming for the BBC programme *Animal Park*. Don's dowsing also revealed a large network of tunnels and waterways under Frome itself and a rudimentary map was produced.

Nunney Castle is said to have at least three tunnels, one to the east heading towards Frome (described above), a second tunnel comes out in fields to the west, and another, explored but now permanently flooded, goes under the river towards The George pub.

At the height of the Cold War local authorities were instructed to take precautions against a nuclear attack. Civil Defence bunkers were to be constructed in strict secrecy and the exact location of most remains a mystery, but it was common local knowledge that one was situated on the outskirts of town near to the modern Wallington Way.

Constructed for the Royal Observer Corps in 1962, it was abandoned in 1991. A Frome master mason, who cannot be named here under the terms of the Official Secrets Act, remembers being interviewed by officers of MI5 concerning the bricking up of bunker entrances in the event of an attack in order to protect their select occupants from nuclear fallout and to keep out the general public.

DID YOU KNOW?
The name Frome derives from the ancient British word 'Fraww' meaning 'brisk' and describes the river; the somewhat sluggish river we see today is the result of the river being deepened as part of flood prevention measures. There are five River Fromes in the South West of England. What people know as the river, flowing alongside Willow Vale, is not the river at all, but a leat cut to serve the town mill in the seventeenth century. The river flowed through what is now Marks and Spencer's car park and traces still remain. The two watercourses rejoin near the Blue House.

St John's Church in the heart of Frome has lost its catacombs. The vaulted cellars must be somewhere under the church, but, despite much searching, no entrance can be found. The only clue we have comes from the late Eunice Overend, who recalled the occasion when workmen relaying the road at the bottom of Gentle Street accidently broke through into the vaults. Prepared for all eventualities, Eunice had a torch with her and she was able to make out details of several tombs before the hole was quickly covered over again. The catacombs await rediscovery; a patch of tarmac on which snow never settles, which implies the ground is hollow beneath, might be the best clue we have.

Buried in the church grounds is a large cistern that collects water from the many springs that emerge on the slopes above the church. This cistern feeds the leat that runs down the middle of Cheap Street, thus ensuring it never runs dry. After disappearing

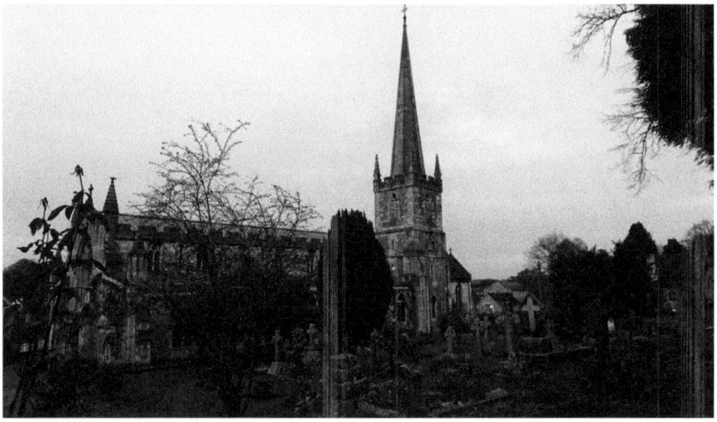

St John's Church was extensively remodelled in the late nineteenth century. (Gary Kearley)

under the pavement, the water eventually comes out alongside the medieval road under the town bridge, before flowing into the river near to Frome Library.

DID YOU KNOW?
Many Frome youngsters learnt to swim at the Victoria Baths off Rook Lane, on land formerly used as an iron foundry. Opened in 1899 at a cost of £1,550 and paid for by public subscription, they closed in 1974. Much of the infrastructure is still there, however, covered by the gardens of the row of picturesque cottages that line the west side of Bath Street. One of the cottages has the changing rooms and boiler house buried under the back lawn, still accessible via a hidden staircase.

The attractive drinking fountain below the church is directly above another of Frome's many tunnels. This was said to have been constructed to allow members of one of the town's wealthy families to enter St John's privately each Sunday, without having to mix with the commoners at the front of the church. Leading from what is now a shop on the opposite corner, it runs under the road, under the churchyard, and into the church where the family no doubt had its own private pews. The entrances have long since been concealed, but the tunnel's existence was confirmed as recently as 2017 by the woman whose job it was, once a week, to sweep the tunnel and the steps leading to and from it to ensure the ladies in the party did not dirty their Sunday best.

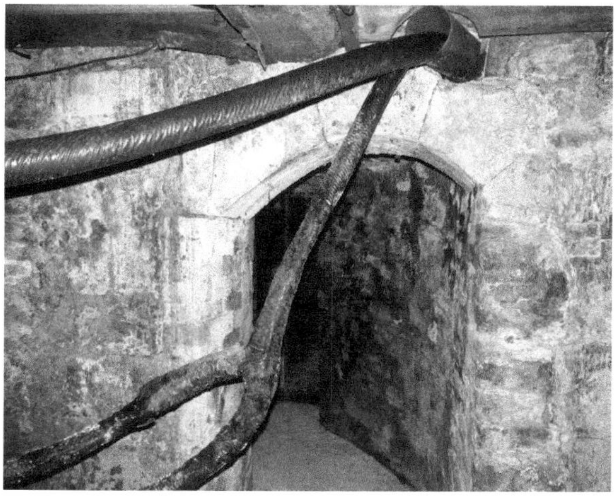

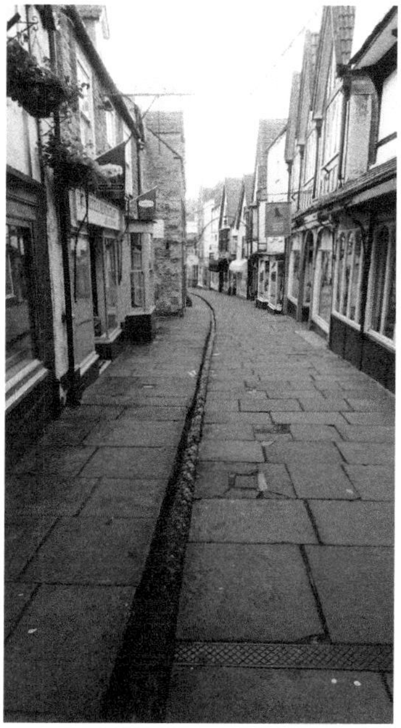

Above: Medieval doorway in Wheatsheaves cellar, partially obscured by modern pipework. (Gary Kearley)

Right: Cheap Street leat, reputed to never run dry. (Gary Kearley)

2. Protest, Rebellion and War

Over the centuries Frome has played its part in most national, and some international, conflicts. Close to Frome, on the southern edge of Selwood Forest, Alfred's Tower is in the vicinity of the place where, in 878, King Alfred is said to have met the men of Somerset, Wiltshire and Hampshire prior to fighting, and defeating, the Danes at the battle of Edington. The Vikings though had their revenge, destroying the monastery at Frome in around AD 1000.

Up until 1380, the local authorities would be heavily fined if someone was murdered in their area, but this fine would be waived if it could be proven that the victim was English. 'Englishry', as it was known, dates back to Norman times when the killing of an Englishman, as opposed to a Norman, was of little consequence. Thus, when one William Plente was killed in Frome, extensive but ultimately unsuccessful efforts were made to prove that he was English in order to avoid the fine.

Frome avoided direct involvement in the Wars of the Roses. Despite the chronic political upheavals and warfare of the second half of the fifteenth century, this was a time of considerable prosperity for the town: just months before the first of multiple battles, that of St Albans in 1455, the first stone bridge over the river was completed. The war came closest to Frome in 1471 when outriders from Queen Margaret's Lancastrian army, marching north from Exeter, were sent into Selwood Forest, at least as far as Bruton, as a decoy to persuade Edward IV, the Yorkist king who was pursuing them, that she was heading east towards London and not north to join forces with Jasper Tudor. Edward arrived in Somerset at Bath before tracking Margaret down and defeating the Lancastrians in a decisive battle at Tewkesbury before she could cross the River Severn and escape into Wales. Thomas Champneys of Frome was heavily fined in the 1490s for supporting Perkin Warbeck, the Yorkist 'pretender', posing as one of the 'Princes in the Tower', the ill-fated sons of Edward IV.

DID YOU KNOW?

Frome has a long tradition of weapon making. When Henry IV took the crown from Richard II in 1400 several prominent Frome citizens were fined for helping to arm Richard's defeated army and were ordered to surrender the lances and axes that had been 'newly made by men of Frome'.

The religious upheavals of the sixteenth century seem to have had limited effect on the day-to-day life in the town. Vicar Thomas Phillips at St John's Church held onto his office through the turbulent reigns of four Tudor monarchs who wrought and fought England's Reformation: Henry VIII, Edward VI, Mary I and Elizabeth I. However, not everyone was prepared to give up their Roman Catholic faith and, in 1549, the Cornish rose in rebellion against the introduction of the Common Prayer Book. This 'Western Rebellion' spread to Devon but was soon put down with great loss of life. Captured rebels were dispersed throughout the area and it was the lot of the Sheriff for Somerset and Dorset, Sir John Thynne, the man who later rebuilt Longleat House, to punish those sent to him. At least one was hanged, drawn and quartered in Frome where payment was made 'for the execution: for irons; for wood for fire to burn the entrails; and a pan or trivet to seethe the limbs'. Masses continued to be held in private houses, accounting, some say, for priest holes that are said to be found throughout the town, including the older houses above St John's on Gentle Street. This tradition can be found in many parts of the country – legends that are notoriously difficult to prove historically. The one in the Chantry, McGarvie has suggested, probably served a less romantic role as a dry larder. The house is an interesting one – said to have been the Marquess of Bath's town house – but it is dated to the late seventeenth century, much too late to have anything to do with the Elizabethan persecution of Jesuit priests. In the Somerset Historic Environment Record the entry for the house is careful to identify the small chamber with a vaulted roof as a 'priest's hole' in inverted commas. Then again, Peter Belham in his *The Making of Frome* claimed 'some fifteen years ago [*c.* 1958] when alterations were being made to "The Chantry" which included the knocking down of some walls, a genuine "priest hole" was found. It was especially fascinating to see the candle grease still on one wall, marking the spot where a small altar had stood'. He concluded it dated from either Elizabeth I's

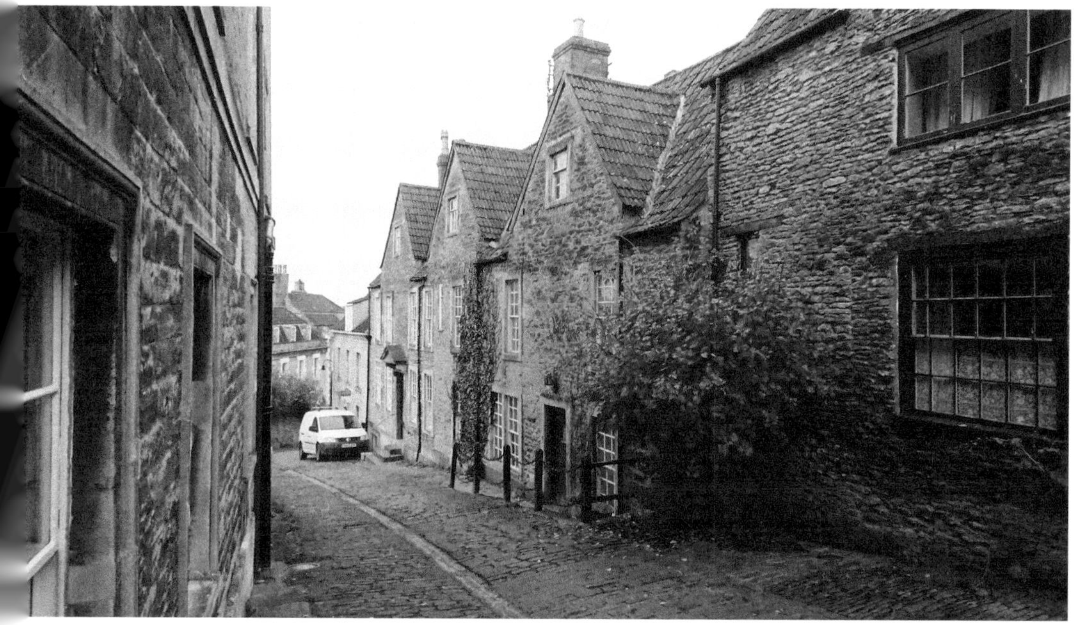

The Chantry in Gentle Street. (Gary Kearley)

reign or even that of her brother and predecessor, Edward VI, who also presided over the persecution of Roman Catholics in the kingdom.

The English Civil War ravaged the country from 1642 to 1651 and the area around Frome saw its share of the action. The town was strongly Puritan and Parliamentarian. The church bells were rung following Roundhead victories and remained silent when the Cavaliers won the day. A certificate issued by Mells solicitor Benjamin Avery confirmed the removal of the idolatrous stained-glass windows in St John's. Local landowners on the other hand were staunch Royalists. Witham House was the home of Sir Ralph Hopton, who commanded the king's army in the west, Woodhouse Castle near Horningsham was the seat of the Royalist Arundel family, Nunney Castle was held for the king by Colonel Richard Prater, and Longleat belonged to another king's man, Sir James Thynne. These Royalist strongholds naturally came to the attention of Cromwell's forces. Witham and Woodhouse were both attacked and taken by Parliamentary forces; Woodhouse was 'slighted' to render it indefensible and twelve of the garrison were hanged, and Nunney was also besieged and ruined by order of Parliament. In addition to sieges there were several skirmishes including Major Francis Duet's surprise dawn raid on Leigh on Mendip that led to the capture of dozens of Royalist troops billeted there on their way to Frome. Despite the town's Parliamentarian sympathies, Lieutenant-General Hopton deemed it safe enough to quarter his loyal Cornish troops overnight in St John's Church as they passed through the town on their way to Bradford-on-Avon, where they took the bridge on 2 July 1643. After the troops left, Richard Ambrosse was paid two shillings by the churchwardens to clean the inside of the church. Despite the loss of so many Royalist strongholds and the general public's support for Parliament, the king visited the area in 1643 to dine with Sir John Horner, and his son, the future Charles II, dined with Hopton at Witham House the following year. The Lord of Frome, Robert Leversedge, was also an ardent Royalist and as a delinquent (supporter of the king) he was forced to pay a huge fine (called compounding) after the war to recover his confiscated estates. Fined a total of £780 in 1646, the sum was reduced to £140 due to his debts, but it still took him until 1652 to raise the money.

When Oliver Cromwell died in 1658 he was succeeded as Lord Protector by his son Richard Cromwell. Abraham Selfe, Frome's bailiff, and his drummer Richard Weyland led the celebrations for the new incumbent, spending the grand sum of five shillings (25p) on beer and three shillings and six pence (17.5p) on a bonfire. The monarchy was restored in 1660 and Charles II reigned for twenty-five years. On his death, he was succeeded by his Catholic brother James (James VII of Scotland, James II of England) in 1685, but within a matter of months James' rule was challenged by Charles II's illegitimate Protestant son James, Duke of Monmouth. Monmouth landed at Lyme Regis, intending to take the crown. The Constable of Frome, one Robert Smith, posted a notice proclaiming Monmouth to be the true king and the local population supported the handsome young duke's claim. The steward of Longleat, Thomas Allen, wrote to his master in London saying, 'they call him King there [Frome] as confidently as if he had the crown on his head'. The chief rebel recruiter was said to have been 'Sir' John Kidd, a former estate gamekeeper at Longleat who assembled 500 local men at Frome to await their 'Protestant Prince'.

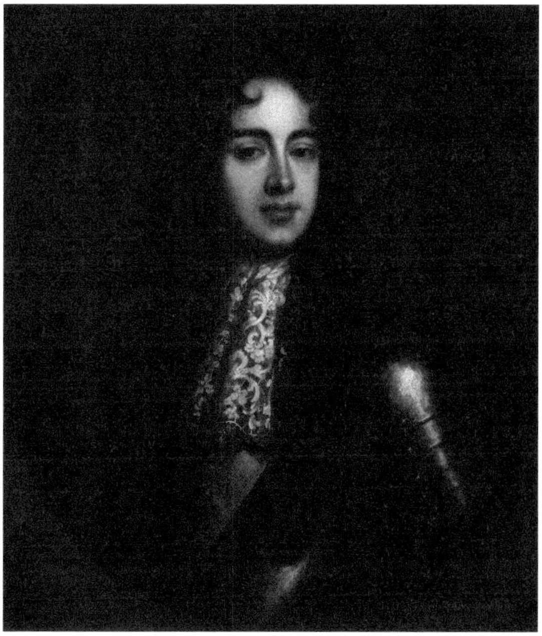

James, Duke of Monmouth.

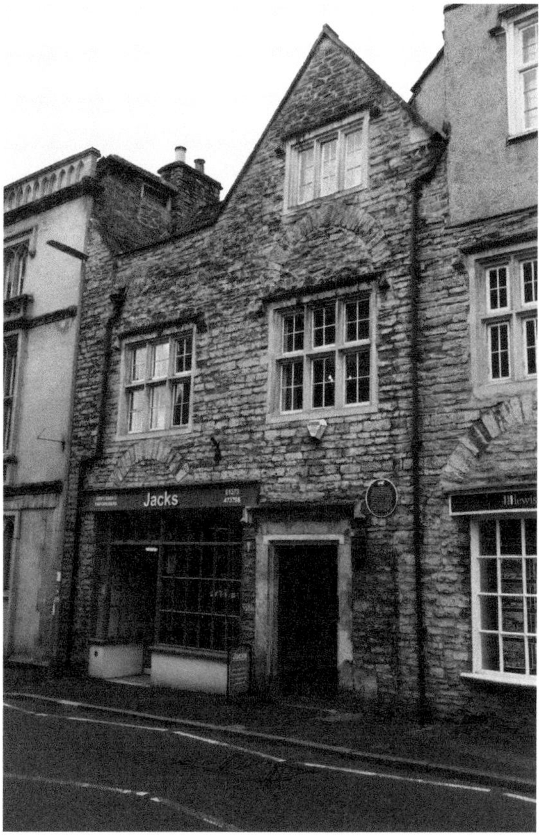

Cork Street, Monmouth's lodgings after the battle of Norton St Philip. (Martin Kearley)

Monmouth arrived at Norton St Philip, just to the north of Frome, on 26 June 1685, and the following day the village saw the penultimate battle fought on English soil with Monmouth's army of artisans and farm labourers winning the fight. Despite the victory, Monmouth decided to fall back to Frome, having been promised that 30,000 recruits and huge quantities of supplies awaited him there. He was to be disappointed as the Earl of Pembroke had brought 160 horse and 30 musketeers to the town soon after Smith had posted the proclamation and dispersed the 1,000 or so potential recruits and confiscated their supplies.

DID YOU KNOW?
When the Normans invaded in 1066 they quickly sought to establish their position and quell any potential rebellion by building castles across the country. Frome had its own Norman motte-and-bailey castle, started in the years immediately after the invasion, but strangely it was never finished. Now known as Hales Castle, this Scheduled Ancient Monument stands in a field just outside East Woodlands and covers the old Roman road from Poole Harbour to Bath.

It was while in Frome, staying at a house in Cork Street, that Monmouth learnt that Archibald Campbell, the Duke of Argyle, who had agreed to support him by simultaneously launching a rebellion in Scotland, had been captured when his small army deserted him after an abortive invasion of lowland Scotland. Monmouth was a broken man and was all for fleeing to the Continent as his army began to drift away from Frome, back to their farms and businesses across the South West. He had to be persuaded by his generals to continue with his campaign, although maybe he should have fled when he could as his army was crushed at the battle of Sedgemoor just a week later. Argyle was executed on 30 June and Monmouth was beheaded on 15 July. Frome's Constable Robert Smith was also condemned; in a letter sent from Whitehall the Earl of Sunderland reported 'his majestie thinks it fit that orders bee given that hee bee hang'd as hee deserves'. In the event the sentence was commuted to deportation to Jamaica to become an 'indentured servant' for ten years. Luckily for Smith all such 'servants' were freed and pardoned in early 1690 following the Glorious Revolution that displaced James II in favour of William and Mary. The infamous Judge Jeffries sentenced 1,381 rebels to death or transportation to the West Indies at the Bloody Assizes. Although fifty-four Frome men were named in the so-called 'roll call of rebels' none were among the twelve men executed on Gibbet Hill in the town at a cost to the Crown of just over £16. These unfortunate victims were hanged then quartered and their remains were displayed at the junction of Butts Hill and Keyford. This gruesome display lived long in the memory of locals, with the site still being marked on the town map nearly a hundred years later, as was the house that Monmouth had lodged in.

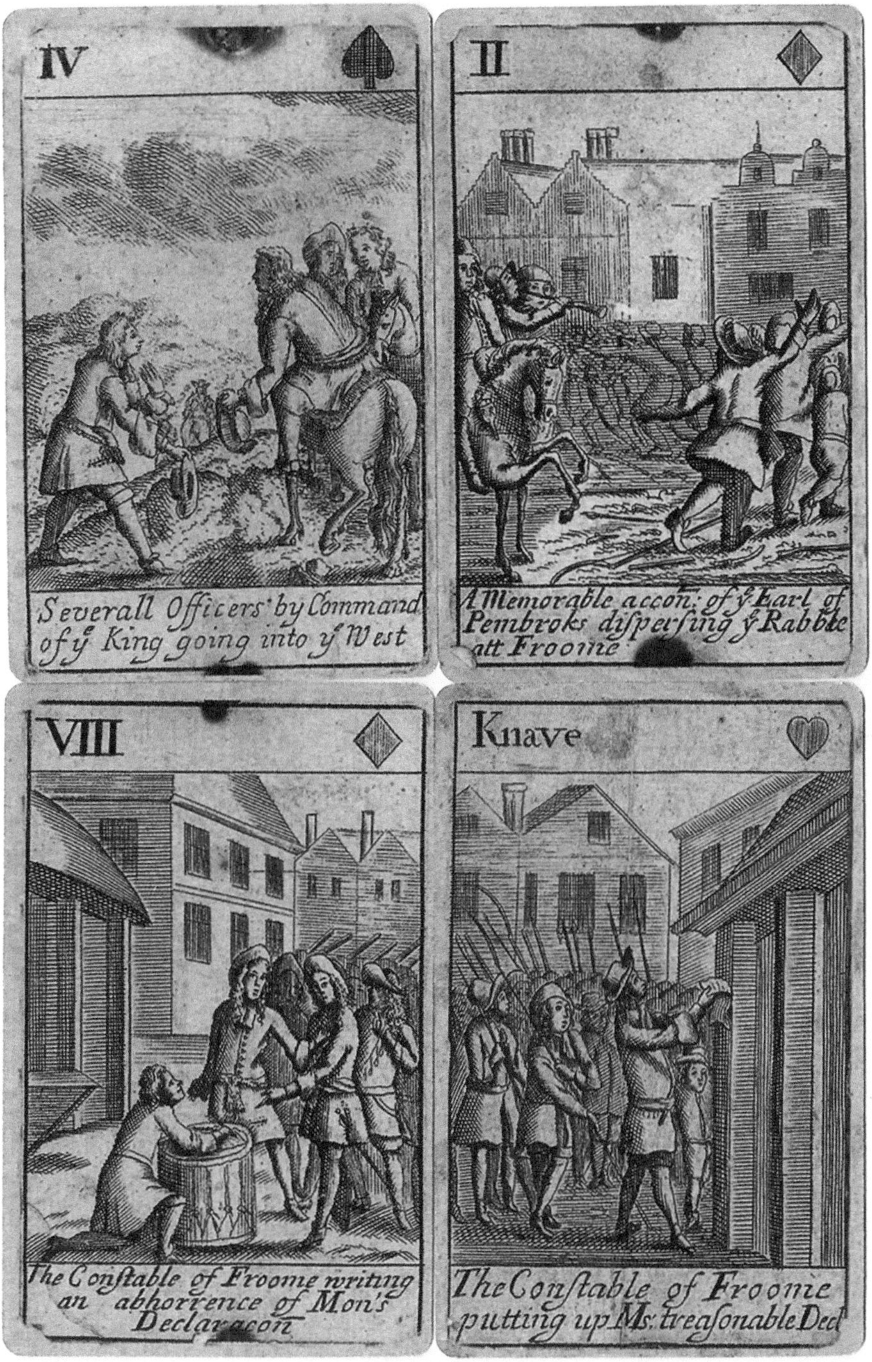

Frome's involvement in the Monmouth Rebellion commemorated in a pack of contemporary playing cards.

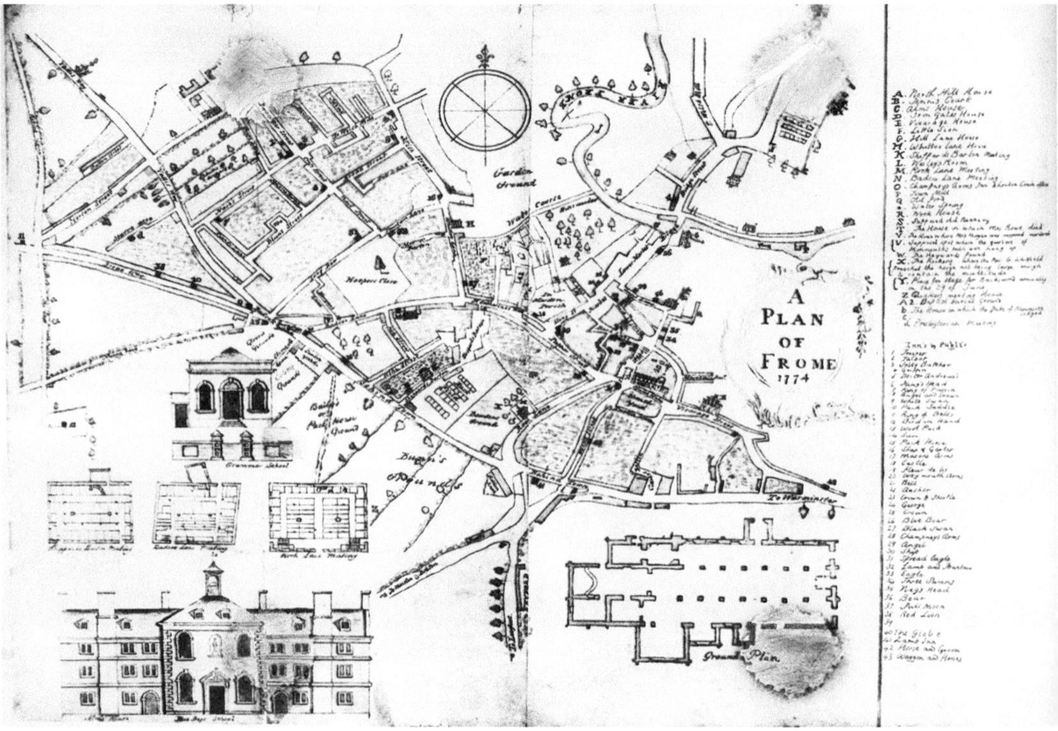

Hand-drawn map of Frome dated 1774.

Before his ill-fated rebellion Monmouth had visited Frome on many occasions, often as a guest of the Thynne family at nearby Longleat, and it is believed that he ordered a house to be built for himself on Catherine Hill on land owned by the Thynnes. If things had turned out differently Frome may well have been able to boast being the home town of James III of England.

Things settled down after the rebellion, but there was still day-to-day crime to deal with and in 1724 a new guardhouse was constructed adjacent to the Blue Boar Inn, replacing the lock-up in the churchyard. In 1798 the churchyard lock-up was reinstated, giving the constables two places of incarceration. It was known as the Blindhouse as it had no windows, with food being lowered down to prisoners through a circular hole in the roof, protected by an iron grill. Both fell into disuse when the new police station was built on Christchurch Street West in 1857. The Blindhouse can still be visited today, although it is now in a very dilapidated state. The lock-up outside the Blue House found a new role as a public convenience until its demolition in the early 1960s.

Despite the best efforts of the volunteer constabulary, criminality abounded. The place became notorious for the clipping of coins and making of counterfeit money. A 'Woodlands groat' at around the start of the eighteenth century was worth fourpence. Lord Weymouth of Longleat had a church built at East Woodlands in 1712 to counter such immoral behaviour and the antiquarian John Collinson was happy to report at the end of the eighteenth century that the church, the respectable business of cutting timber, and the

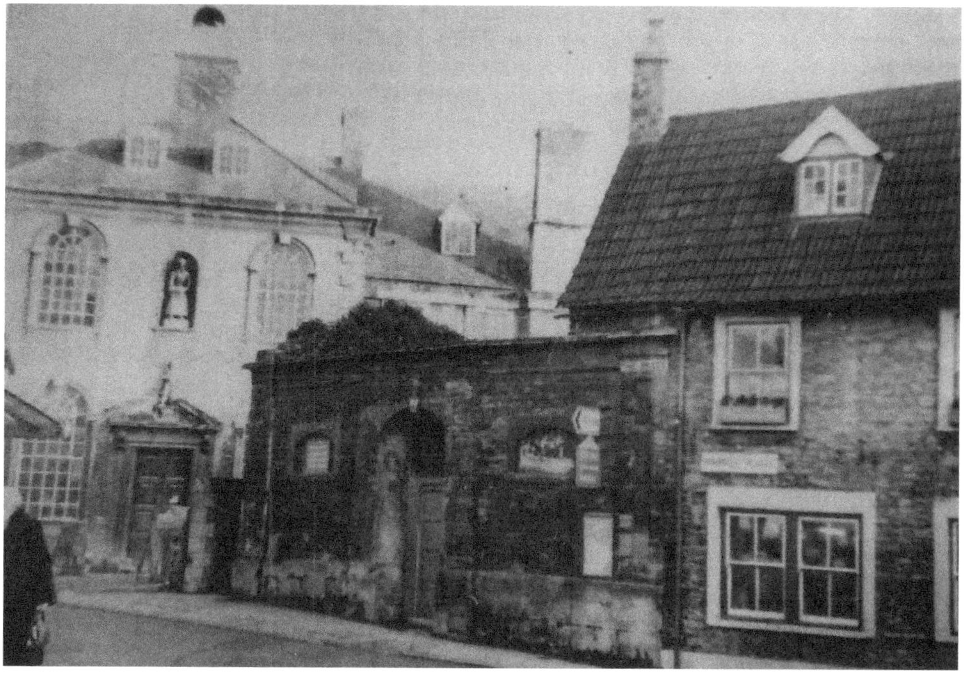

Above: Guardhouse next to the Blue Boar in Market Place.

Right: Entrance to the Blindhouse in St John's churchyard. (Martin Kearley)

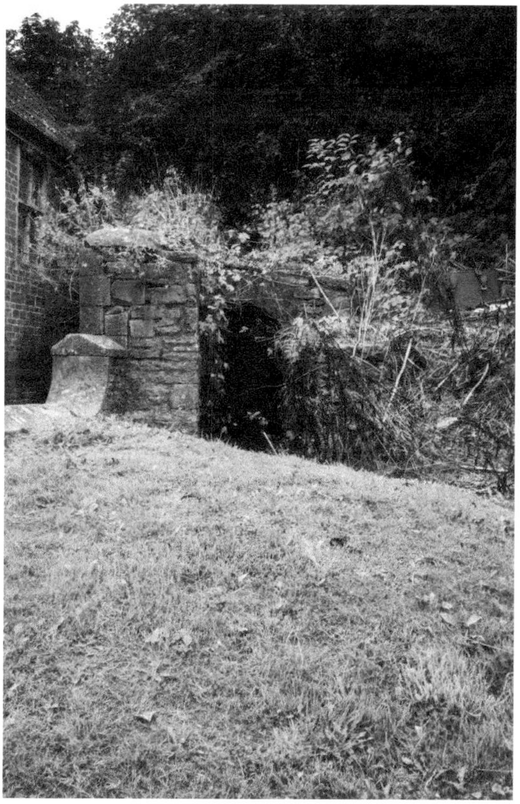

establishment of several small farms had brought an end to the general lawlessness of the area and drawn its inhabitants to 'honest and useful labour'.

The town was rife with low-level criminality. On 20 December 1817 a local boy was found hiding in a shop in King Street, belonging to a Mr West, intent on stealing the till. The boy claimed he had been coerced into it by a lad from Bath. Both were brought before the local Justice of the Peace, the Reverend H. Sainsbury. Although Sainsbury released the local boy, he ordered the other 'to be whipped through the town', a sentence which the constable was happy to 'put in force'. There was no professional police force and law and order was maintained by locally appointed, unpaid constables. One such constable was Isaac Gregory, a somewhat reluctant officer of the law as his duties often brought him into conflict with many of the people he knew as valued customers at his leather-working business on Cheap Street. He kept a detailed record of his time in office – an exceptionally rich historical record of life in Regency-era Frome, which has been transcribed by Michael McGarvie and published by the Frome Society for Local Study. After an incident at the Ship Inn on Badcox ('The Artisan' at the time of this publication) one of the drinkers Gregory was forced to eject told him that his actions would 'lose the selling of £20 worth of leather'. Appointed by the Earl of Cork and Orrery at the annual court leet held at the George Hotel, he served two terms, 1813–14 and 1817–18. His first term coincided with the Napoleonic Wars. Gregory had the difficult, time-consuming job of allocating billets for the yeomanry and other troops passing through the town, having to deal with disgruntled locals who did not want them in their homes. He was also required by law to commandeer wagons for the movement of supplies, often officers' baggage, which interrupted the logging activities in Selwood Forest, and to ensure that law and order was maintained during the balloting for militia duty. All of this was on top of his normal policing duties which mainly revolved around theft, domestic violence and breaking up fights in the town's many pubs, most often near to closing time (10.00 p.m.). The George on Market Place was often the scene of fights being the only pub in town to charge less than sixpence (2.5p) for a quart of strong beer, attracting what Gregory called 'a great influx of Blackguards to the house'. This heavy drinking often led to bloodshed, especially on market days.

In addition to consigning drunks to the lock-up for excessive drinking on the Sabbath, another of Gregory's Sunday duties was to tour the fields and send to church any children he found playing there. Constable Gregory would have been familiar with the pillory that once stood at the top of the upper Market Place, used for the last time in 1814 to punish Gideon Hill who was pelted with rotten vegetables after being charged for keeping a house of ill-repute.

Frome elected its first Member of Parliament as a consequence of the 1832 Reform Act and this provoked a bout of extreme violence in the town. The election was held in the Market Place on 10 December 1832 and it was a straight fight between a local clothier, Thomas Sheppard, representing the Radical Party, and the owner of Orchardleigh, Sir Thomas Champneys, standing for the Tories. Sheppard was pelted with stones while giving a speech on the hustings and a man died in the clash between the two sets of supporters, many of whom were armed. The Riot Act was read from the balcony of

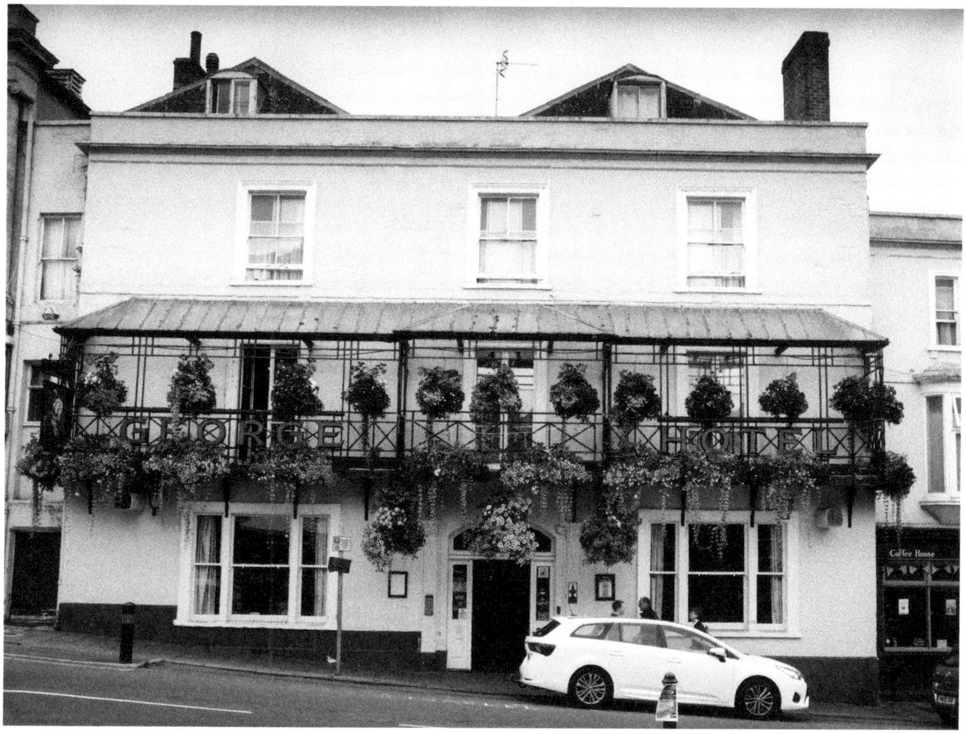

The George, Market Place. (Martin Kearley)

the George and the constables shot into the crowd using carbines borrowed from the yeomanry, bringing down two of the rioters. The constables were led by a Frome man, Captain Wickham of the North Somerset Yeomanry, who is said to have bravely charged into the mob, despite being wounded in the melee. Ironically, most of those involved were not eligible to vote due to the restricted enfranchisement represented by the Reform Act; they were there, risking their lives, to serve the interests of their employer or landlord respectively. Champney was forced to retreat to Fromefield House where he took refuge for three weeks. He was well protected – the household provided hot meals for 300 of his supporters every night of what amounted to a siege. The final result of the election? A victory for Sheppard by 163 votes to 100.

This disturbance was only the latest in a series of riots for which the town had gained quite a reputation. The first recorded riot occurred in 1444 when Robert Leversedge of Vallis Manor House entered the town with an armed mob, intent on resolving a dispute with the Earl of Ormond, a major property owner in Frome. The earl was not at home, but his wife and son were and they were both thrown onto the pavement as Leversedge's men ran amok, seizing properties, attacking the earl's supporters and setting up barricades on all approach roads to stop reinforcements. Church records from the period noted such violence and shedding of blood in the immediate vicinity of the church that all services had to cease until the people could be 'reconciled'. Nevertheless, despite the disorder of

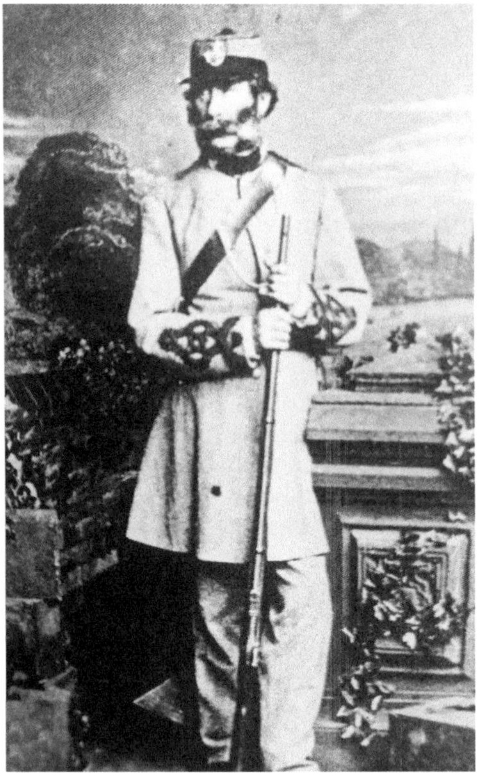

Major Wickham in the uniform of the Frome Selwood Volunteers, *c.* 1870.

the mid-fifteenth century, the Leversedge family maintained their standing and were still lords of the manor 300 years later.

There was rioting against high taxation in 1649, but on this occasion, according to local report, the protesters were not the usual 'scum and malignants of the town'. The rioting of disgruntled weavers in Frome, some of whom seem to have come from cloth-making towns in neighbouring Wiltshire, was reported in *The London Journal* in 1726. Their activities were suppressed by 'a troop of Dragoons', the ringleaders incarcerated in the gaols at Ilchester (Somerset) and Salisbury (Wiltshire).

Another disturbance followed when Frome men were selected for the militia in 1813. Enrolment into the militia during the Napoleonic War was so unpopular that names had to be drawn by ballot. Two of the men chosen became so disorderly that they had to be removed to the town gaol. Their friends objected to this and marched on the gaol, attempting to free those inside by taking the roof off. Peace was only restored when the Riot Act was read. There was yet more trouble in the town around this time when a mob, said to be 5,000-strong, set off for Sheppard's Mill at Spring Gardens intent on destroying the new power looms that threatened to put the town's weavers out of work. Having seized five looms, the mob proceeded towards the town centre where they intended to burn them. Unfortunately for these southern contemporaries of the more famous 'Luddite' machine-breakers in the industrial north, forty special constables had been hidden in the yard of the Wheatsheaves pub on Bath Street and as the procession passed

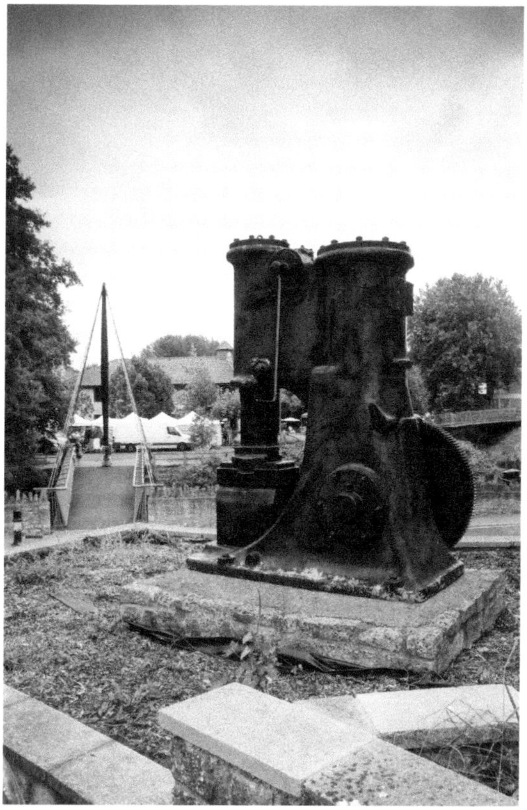

Right: Henley Way, a reminder of Frome's industrial past. (Martin Kearley)

Below: Entrance to Wheatsheaves yard, scene of Luddite-style violence. (Martin Kearley)

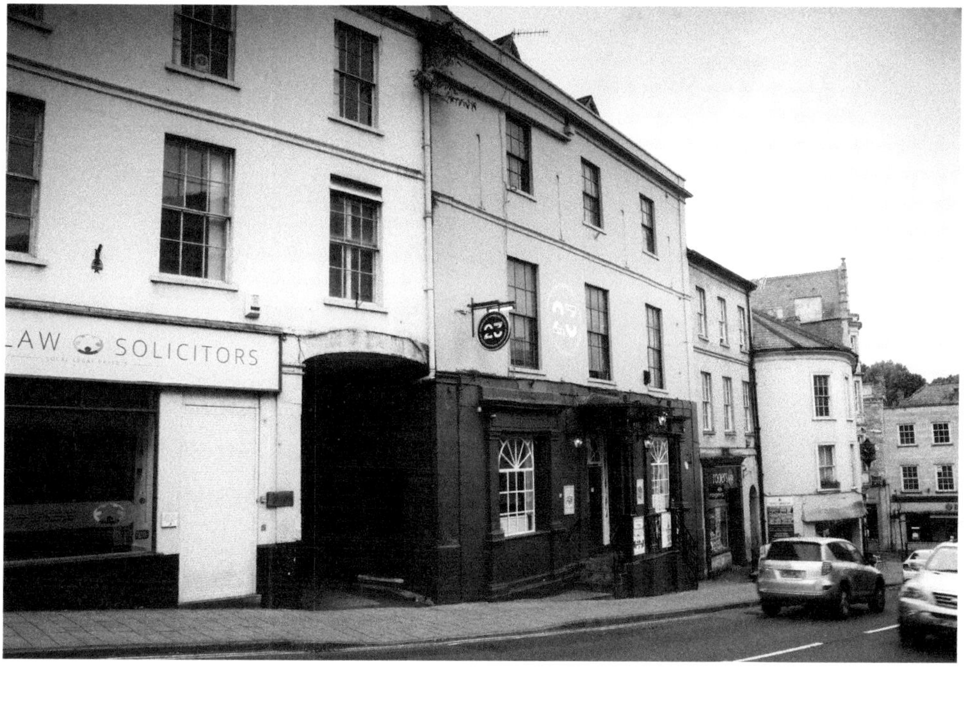

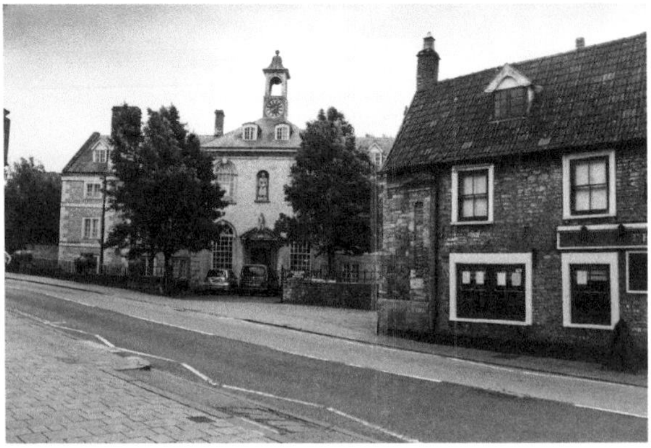

Blue House and Blue Boar showing remains of the guardhouse on the pub wall. (Martin Kearley)

they rushed out and dragged the looms and their bearers into the yard, slamming the gates behind them. The crowd only dispersed when the Riot Act was read and muskets were aimed at them from the windows of the upper stories of the pub.

In 1867 there were further riots in the town following the posting of leaflets calling on the population to gather in the Market Place to 'use endeavours to put down the price of food', the price of bread having risen to 7½*d* (3.5p) for a 4 lb (1.8 kg) loaf. The authorities were ready for trouble and 200 special constables were sworn in and forty policemen from the County Constabulary arrived by train on the recently opened railway. Stones and bottles were thrown by the crowd of 2,000–3,000 and the situation was getting out of hand. Once more the Riot Act was read outside the Blue Boar and the crowd eventually dispersed when, according to the *Somerset and Wiltshire Journal* at the time, the chief constable warned them 'if another stone were thrown he would let the police loose upon them, and then he would not like to be in their skins.'

A report dated 1848 revealed that the North Somerset Yeomanry had assembled in full in aid of civil authorities seven times since it was inaugurated in 1797 and that different troops and detachments had been called out sixty-four times for the same purpose. While these figures cover the whole of the troops' geographical area, it is indicative of the general lawlessness of the times and the reliance of the civil authorities on the volunteer army.

DID YOU KNOW?
During the Second World War 1.5 million children were evacuated from major cities to the countryside and several ended up in Frome. Volunteers would visit the church halls in which the children were temporarily housed to choose which children to take in. Several of the evacuees described the selection process as similar to a cattle market. It was not only people who were evacuated, entire factories were relocated to the country to protect their vital work from enemy bombers. The engineering company G. E. Evans was moved to Frome from Portsmouth and the aircraft manufacturers Rotol from Cheltenham.

The Second World War saw more violence in the town, although it was nothing to do with the Nazis. In the build-up to D-Day allied troops were stationed at Marston House, Longleat and Orchardleigh and would come into town for the pubs and, it was said, for the local girls. The Australian and New Zealand troops became notorious for starting fights in the Market Place. Worse still were the battles between black and white American troops. This got to be so bad that Frome was forced to introduce its own brand of segregation, with black and white troops only allowed into town on different days, American military police and British 'bobbies' patrolling together to ensure compliance. At least one German serviceman did make it to Frome when, on the night of 5 July 1941, a Heinkel HeIII bomber was shot down by an RAF Beaufighter over Vallis Farm at Great Elm. One of the crew of the downed plane, Gefreiter Ludwig Kugal, survived the crash but after hiding for some hours he walked into town and surrendered himself to the local police. Two other crew members were captured but records do not show if they too were kept in Frome police station.

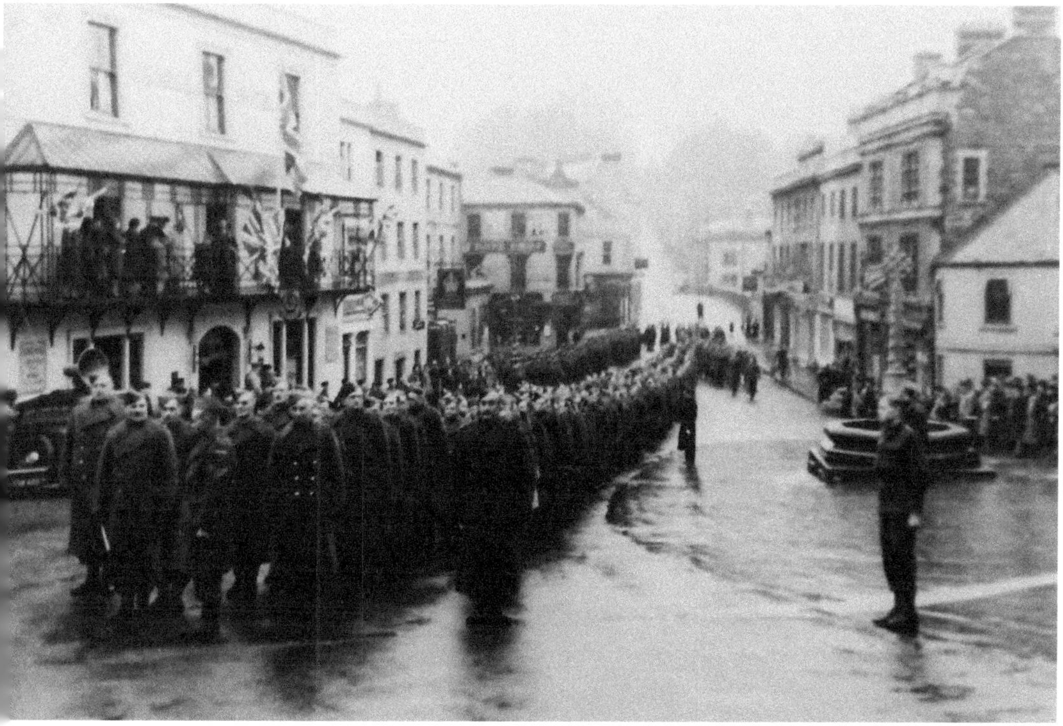

Troops parade in Market Place during the Second World War.

3. The Witches of Selwood

Rode revel, Beckington rout
The Devil's in Frome and they can't get him out.
(Old Frome rhyme collected by folklorists Ruth Tongue and Kingsley Palmer)

Anyone with a passing interest in English witchcraft belief will be familiar with Lancashire's Pendle Forest witch hunts, but few, even among those who live here, are aware of the equally rich witchcraft history of Selwood Forest. If we stretch the medieval bounds of the royal forest a little to the west to include Shepton Mallet and south to include the parish of Stoke Trister, the northern boundary of which meets the forest at Trister Gate, we have a small parcel of land that extends no more than 20 miles north to south (Beckington to Stoke Trister) and about 15 west to east (Shepton to Rode) in which can be found a remarkable amount of evidence for witchcraft-related activity. It is closely associated with the publication of a couple of the most influential demonologists writing in the English language (the most famous of which was written in Frome), it was the location, allegedly, of several witch covens, and in it we find exceptionally detailed records of the rough treatment of six 'witches' in three 'swimming' episodes in the space of forty years. The tales and associated texts emanating from the area were of great importance in the final great debate in elite circles concerning the reality of demonic spirits and their witch acolytes until, for most, it was resolved, or merely abandoned, in the eighteenth century.

Between 1662 and 1672, when Joseph Glanvill was the incumbent of St John's Church in Frome, installed by the Thynne family of Longleat, he started work on what would eventually become his monumental *Saducismus Triumphatus, or Full and Plain Evidence, concerning Witches and Apparitions, in two Parts, the First treating of their Possibility, and the Second of their real Existence,* completed and published by Henry More, Glanvill's fellow member of and greatest ally in the Royal Society, in 1681, a year after the author's death. This famous work included the evidence gleaned from a 'book of examinations' kept by an eminent local magistrate Robert Hunt. Hunt supplied Glanvill with five 'relations' concerning the activities of numerous witches in the area around Frome. These included detailed accounts of sabbat meetings – a common enough phenomenon in other European cases but exceptionally rare in the English record.

Glanvill has long been recognised as the towering figure in the witchcraft debates of the later seventeenth century, albeit remembered primarily for being on what modern sensibility is prone to consider the wrong side. 'It is strange fortune of some men to be immortalised by their follies rather than by their virtues', his nineteenth-century biographer remarked, in reference to 'his ardent advocacy of a dying superstition'. In

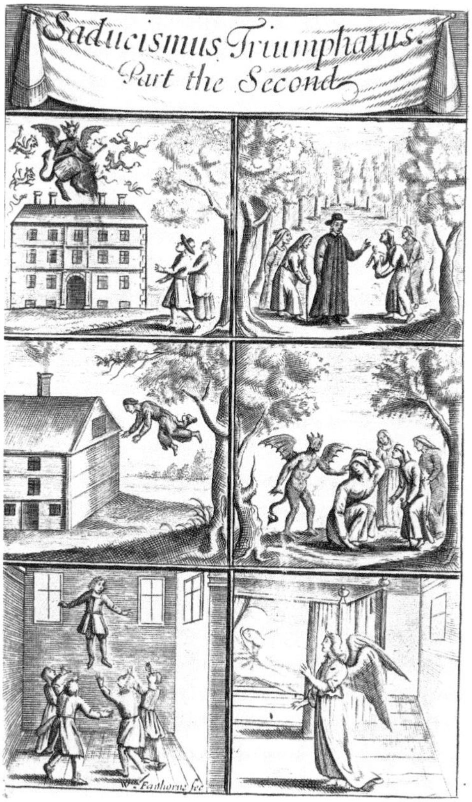

Joseph Glanvill, *Saducismus Triumphatus* (1681), frontispiece showing scenes of paranormal activity in and around Selwood Forest.

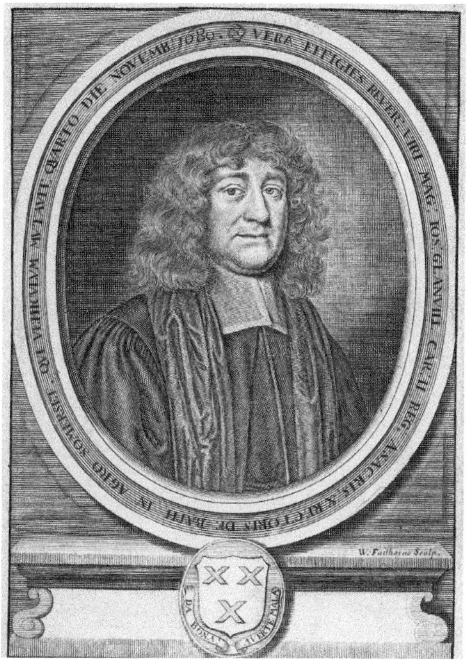

Joseph Glanvill, vicar of Frome Selwood, 1662–72.

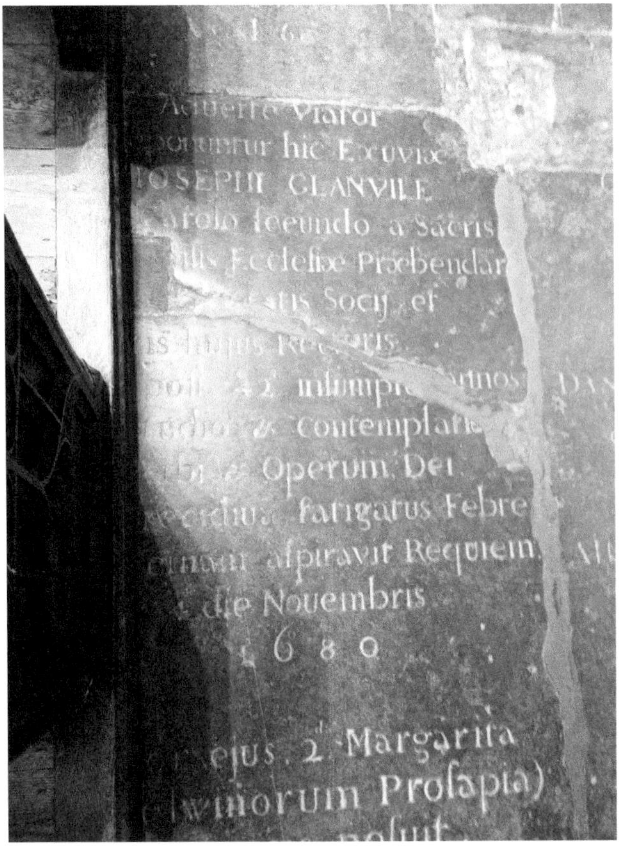

Joseph Glanvill's memorial stone in Bath Abbey.

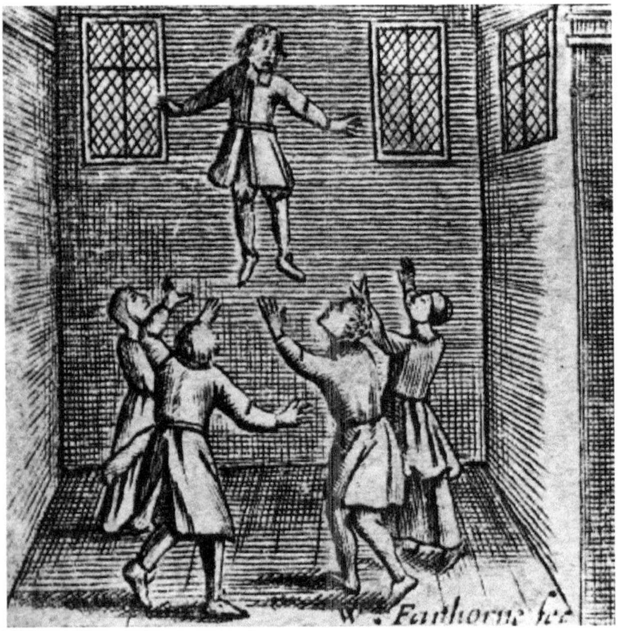

The levitation of Richard Jones, 1658.

fact, Glanvill was a most progressive thinker and, as a member of the Royal Society, and from 1670 secretary of its short-lived Somerset branch, one keenly interested in the society's revelations of mechanical 'laws' as an antidote to atheism – proof of divine and immaterial forces at work in nature. His was a scientific demonology entirely in keeping with Restoration science. From his home in Frome his contribution to the witchcraft debate in England in the later seventeenth century was of colossal importance both in provoking the scepticism of some of his readers and invoking the credulity of others. He spearheaded the final campaign within the English intelligentsia to face down the 'sadducees' and 'atheists', making further waves in the wake of the radical publications of Thomas Hobbes, originally a Wiltshire man who came from Malmesbury, 30 miles north of Frome. Whether, in so doing, Glanvill helped perpetuate witch hunting in England or speeded its decline is uncertain. No study of the demise of the English witch hunt is complete without careful consideration of Glanvill's contribution.

The first witchcraft case in the region that Joseph Glanvill related concerned the trial of Jane Brooks of Shepton Mallet in 1658. Richard Jones first met Jane Brooks one Sunday afternoon in November 1657. Richard, 'a sprightly youth about twelve years old', saw her peering in through the windows of the Jones family home. He opened the door to her and, in return for a piece of bread, she gave him an apple and then, ominously, 'stroked him down on the right side, shook him by the hand, and bade him good night'. On the following Monday evening Richard Jones roasted and ate the apple Brooks had given him and promptly became extremely ill with symptoms that included fitting. Eyewitnesses claimed to have seen the boy levitate. Fairly swiftly there was talk of black magic in the town. Following her identification as the beggar who had given the lingering child the cursed apple, Brooks and her sister, Alice Coward, were arrested and interrogated by Hunt and another very active Justice of the Peace at this time, John Cary, at Castle Cary on 8 December 1657. Jones appeared before them again in January in Shepton Mallet and also in February when 'many gentlemen, ministers and others' were also present. The case had caused quite a stir. In the courtroom, as on previous occasions, the lad put on a good show: 'The boy fell into his fit upon the sight of Jane Brooks, and lay in a man's arms like a dead person.' The parish register for Shepton reveals he died in February the following year. The case was referred to the Chard assizes where Brooks was found guilty and, eventually, hanged.

DID YOU KNOW?

The activities of witch hunters in the vicinity of Frome and Selwood Forest brought about the death, by execution, incarceration, or misadventure of at least three of their targets. The region, it was claimed, was home to a 'hellish knot' of witches, for which we have more than thirty names for the period 1658–94, many of whom can be traced in local records.

In chronological terms the next of the cases associated with Selwood Forest in the *Saducismus* is Glanvill's 'Relation VIII', which concerns a trial at Taunton in 1663. It is based on the record of October 1672 made by 'Mr Pool, a servant and officer in the court to Judge Archer, in his Circuits'. Although the account does not indicate in which part of Somerset Julian Cox lived, an editorial postscript in the *Saducismus* Henry More reveals she was examined by Robert Hunt before her case was heard at Taunton. This strongly implies that she lived within the area of his jurisdiction – in other words within, or close to, Selwood Forest.

Pool recorded the extraordinary tale of a seventy-year-old, pipe-smoking witch called Julian Cox, who could turn herself into a hare and had a monstrous toad familiar. Cox was indicted for witchcraft 'which she practiced on a young maid, whereby her body languished, and was impaired of health by reason of strange fits'. When the girl answered the door to Cox she incurred the fury of the old woman by refusing her alms. Cox told her she would regret her action before night fell. Shortly afterwards she began suffering fits and had visions of Cox from whom she implored others in the house to save her. The rest of the household became convinced she really was bewitched after the girl seized a knife and cut the leg of the witch, a manifestation that none but her could see. Julian Cox was found at her home with a freshly wounded leg she had recently bandaged. After this the young woman claimed she was forced by the witch to swallow pins. For a whole day she was seen eating her invisible pins and by the evening she was in agony, screaming in pain, as 'in several parts of the girl's body great swellings appeared, and out of the head of the swellings several great pins' points appeared'. Mr Pool declared thirty of these pins were presented before the court at Taunton, some of which he had handled himself.

The account asserts that Cox was around seventy years old in the early 1660s. A search of several hundred parish registers for Somerset for baptismal records of a Julian Cox or someone with a similar name has produced just three results for the period between 1680 and 1710. One of these is male, one, Julian Coxe, born in Bath in 1596, is female, and the sex of a third, Julian Coxe, born in Nunney, in the Frome Hundred, on 6 June 1591, is not recorded. If this Julian Cox(e) was still alive in the early 1660s he/she would have just turned seventy. Of course there is every reason to suppose our Julian Cox is remembered by her married name but a search of the parish records for marriages between 1605 and 1640 in the county of well over 200 men and women with Cox or Coxe in their baptismal surname does not produce a single one with the name Julian or something similar (other than the occasional Anne). Incidentally, a surprisingly high proportion of women in this period remained unmarried throughout their adult lives. The chances of the Nunney child being the witch in the account are slight but certainly not out of the question. There might even be some historical truth in the local tradition that Nunney's picturesque fourteenth-century castle was the setting of several witch trials and that it is haunted by the ghost of a woman hanged for witchcraft.

Hunt alluded to another Selwood witchcraft case in a letter dated 26 February 1665: 'a young maid died at Kilmington on Wednesday, bewitched by an apple, lay three weeks in great torment and died Wednesday, her body broke and her bowels came out.' Kilmington, a few miles south of Frome, is at the southern end of the forest. Hunt continued, 'The story is too long for this paper. This unhappy business of witches has given me very much

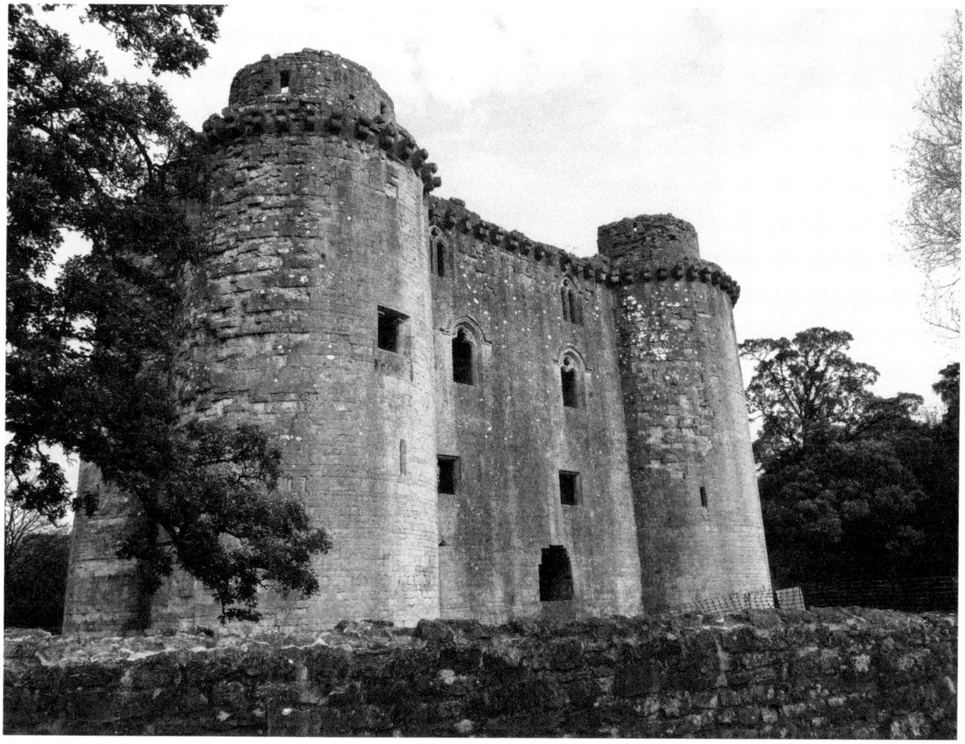

Above: Nunney Castle, said to be haunted by the ghost of a hanged witch. (Andrew Pickering)

Right: A sabbat meeting in Selwood Forest.

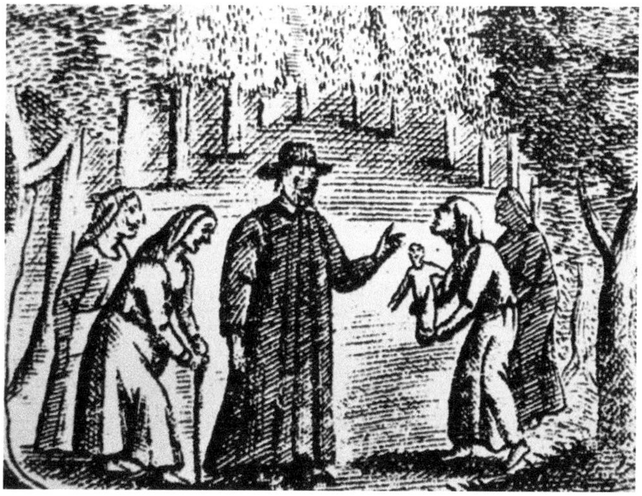

trouble and they have done very much mischief both to cattle and people, but I suppose some of them will receive their reward and they well deserve it.'

The remaining Hunt-Glanvill narratives set in Selwood Forest and written down for publication by Frome's vicar are the famous and extraordinary histories of the Stoke Trister and nearby Brewham covens and their sabbat meetings. These are unparalleled in the English tradition in the fullness of their accounts of feasting, dancing, and the ritual baptising and piercing with thorns of wax effigies (sometimes known as poppets), which became the instrument of the coven's *maleficia*. Most importantly, they were convened by the Devil who, in the guise of a handsome man in black, led the proceedings. The alleged meetings, at open places in the forest which were probably unenclosed common grounds, could well have had at least something to do with traditional gatherings and activities such as dances on particular holy days. Furthermore, in this Restoration era, nonconformist ministers who had been ejected from their livings might well have attempted to pursue their ministry in such places. As Jonathan Barry has suggested, such men could have been the men in black coordinating the meetings of Selwood's 'witches', which coincided with the passing of the first Conventicle Act in 1644 that forbade meetings for religious worship, other than in family prayer, outside of the church. Of particular interest in this context is Edward Bennett, born in South Brewham in 1618. After serving as curate to nearby Batcombe's rector, Richard Bernard, whose *Guide to Grand-Jury Men*, another hugely influential treatise on witchcraft, was first published in 1627 when Bennett was just ten years old, he held a living in Dorset from which he was removed in 1662. In 1665, the year in which the Brewham witches were tried, he spent a couple of months in Ilchester gaol before, ultimately, returning to Brewham, where, in 1672, he was licensed to use his home as a Presbyterian meeting house. Here he was buried the following year. As for Stoke Trister, the most likely candidate is John Batt (1618–73), who was ejected from the living in 1662. In 1665, the very year of the Stoke Trister and Brewham witchcraft trials, Batt was living, and occasionally preaching, at the home of a farmer in the parish.

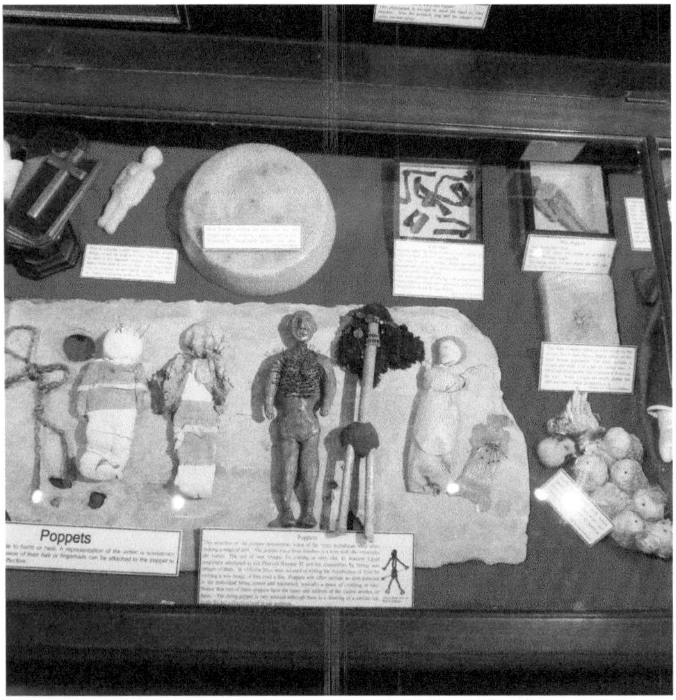

A collection of poppets in the Museum of Witchcraft in Boscastle. (Andrew Pickering)

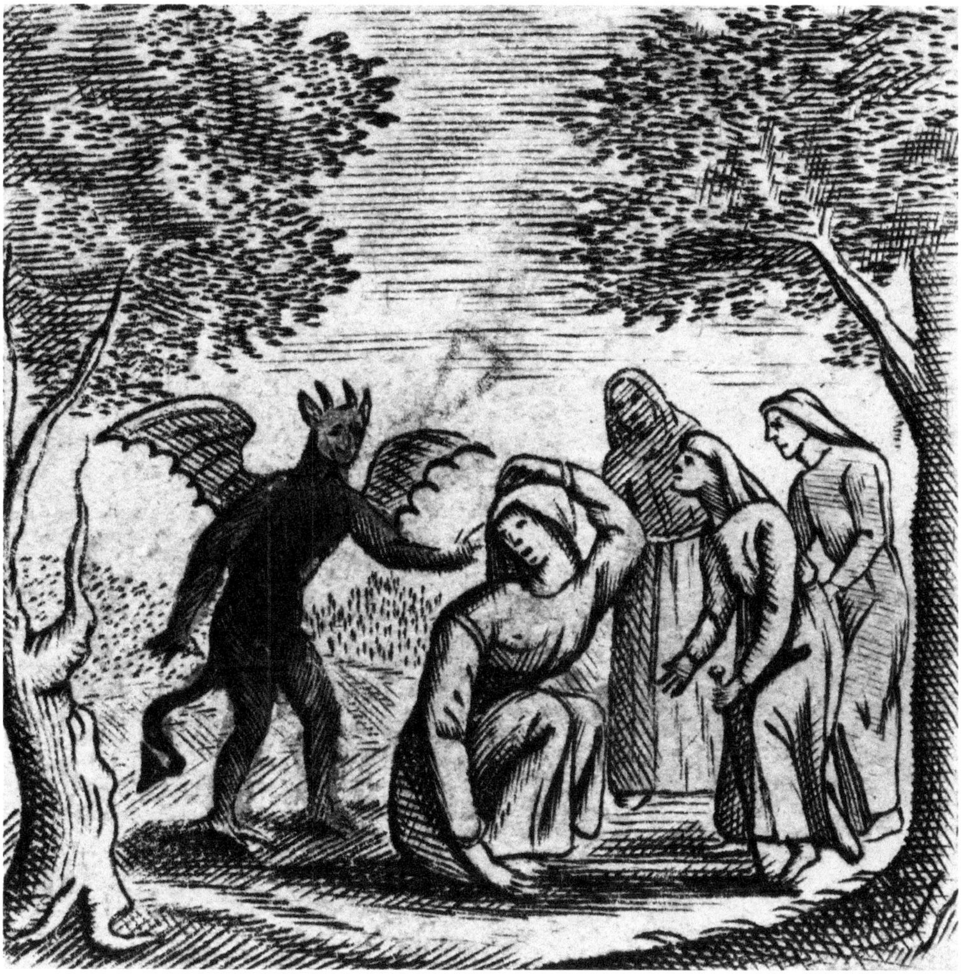

The Devil with the witches of Selwood Forest.

Between 23 January and 15 March 1665, Hunt heard the statements of at least thirteen people across thirteen days of investigation. The sequence of the hearings suggests that his interest in illicit meetings in Stoke Trister somehow prompted similar allegations in Brewham – just as he completed his Stoke Trister enquiries, the Brewham ones began. More than twenty people, some men but mostly women, were recorded in Hunt's examinations as attending the sabbats at various places in the forest. But for some unspecified intervention from above, Hunt's activities were set to become a witch hunt on a scale comparable to that in Pendle Forest in 1612, or even that of Matthew Hopkins, the self-styled 'Witchfinder-General', in the east of England in the mid-1640s. Glanvill deeply regretted the suppressing of Robert Hunt's pursuit of witches in Selwood Forest for, 'had not his discoveries and endeavours met with great opposition and discouragement from some then in authority', he wrote, 'the whole clan of those hellish confederates in these parts might have been justly exposed and punished.'

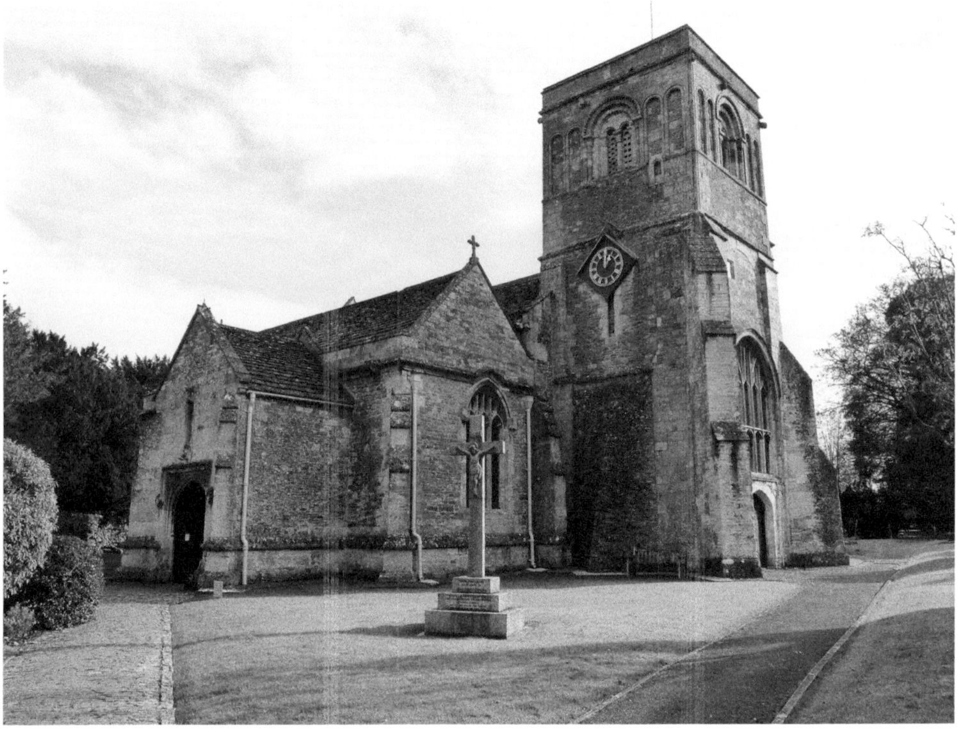

St George's Church, Beckington. (Andrew Pickering)

Four years after what is thought to have been the last execution for witchcraft in England – that of Alice Molland in Exeter in 1685 – more West Country 'witches' were discovered very close to Frome in the village of Beckington and, in 1690, brought to trial at the assize court of Sir John Holt at Taunton. For a time, their case took centre stage in the ongoing debate regarding the reality of witchcraft but it would be largely forgotten in subsequent histories. The earliest account of these events appeared in a double-side broadsheet, printed in London in 1689 under the heading *Great News from the West of England.* In 1691 the puritan polemicist Richard Baxter included a further account of the case, provided by Beckington's rector, Mr May Hill, in his last major work *The Certainty of the Worlds of Spirits.* Baxter, who lived in London, was introduced to Hill by his friend, John Humfrey, who had been the vicar of St John's, Frome, until he was replaced by Joseph Glanvill in 1662. Baxter, in turn, had corresponded with Glanvill on several occasions prior to Glanvill's death in 1680. The Beckington case was not an isolated incident but part of an ongoing campaign of leading clerics, with close connections to each other and also to Frome, to eradicate witchcraft. Most of the protagonists in the case, including the witches and the bewitched, can be identified in the parish registers and other contemporary documents.

The survival of two distinct records of the same episode, albeit probably by the same hand, makes for an exceptionally rich account. The tale begins with the activities of an eighteen-year-old lad, William Spicer, who, 'as he was wont to pass by the Alms-house (where lived an Old Woman, about Four-score) he would call her *Witch,* and tell her of her

Buns', by which he meant her demon familiars. In revenge, the woman 'threatened him with a *Warrant*, and accordingly did fetch one from a Neighbouring *Justice of the Peace*, at which he was so frightened, that he humbled himself to her, and promised never to call her so again'. Nevertheless, 'Within a few days after this Young Man fell into the strangest Fits that ever Mortal beheld with Eyes.' He began to suffer with fits, visions, and bouts of vomiting pins, a curious but prevalent feature of many English witchcraft narratives by this time: 'when he did call for some *Small Beer* to drink, he would be sure to bring up some *Crooked Pins*; first and last, to the Number of Thirty, and upwards.' William Spicer and other family members can be found in the parish records and the author of *Great News* was absolutely correct in suggesting he was around eighteen years old: the son of William and Margaret Spicer, he was baptised on 28 August 1670. He and his several siblings came from a poor family and they had recently been bereaved by the death of their mother, who was buried in the parish in 1687.

DID YOU KNOW?
The most famous account of the most famous poltergeist in the history of early modern England was written in Frome by the vicar of St John's, Joseph Glanvill. It was first published in his book *Some Philosophical Considerations Touching Witches and Witchcraft* (1666) and relates the author's personal experience of disturbing supernatural happenings at a house in Tidworth near Salisbury in 1663.

Another eighteen-year-old, Mary Hill (no relation to May Hill), also made an enemy of Elizabeth Carrier, the old woman accused of bewitching William Spicer, first in a dispute over possession of a ring, next because she refused to accompany her to find spinning work in neighbouring Frome, and, finally, because she denied her the gift of an apple. Mary soon became ill with the same afflictions as William. Her strange vomiting was spectacular:

> she began to throw up *Crooked Pins*, and continued to do so for the space of a Fortnight. After this, she began to throw up *Nails* and *Pins*, and then she ceased for the space of Eight Days. And then she began to throw up *Nails* again, and *Handles* of *Spoons*, both of *Pewter* and *Brass*, several pieces of *Iron*, *Lead*, and *Tin*, with several clusters of *Crooked Pins*, some tied with Yarn and some with Thread, with an abundance of Blood between while; and so she continued to do for some considerable time. She threw up in all, more than Two Hundred *Crooked Pins*, besides several clusters of *Crooked Pins*, Sixteen or Seventeen in a cluster, Seven Pieces of *Pewter*, Four Pieces of *Brass*, being *Handles* of *Spoons*, Six Pieces of *Lead*, some whereof were *Handles* of *Spoons*, and some, the *Lead* of a *Window*, besides one Solid Piece of *Lead*, which weighed full two Ounces; Six long Pieces of *Latten*, with *Wire* belonging to them; Five Pieces of *Iron*, one whereof was round, but hollow, and very big; and Two and Twenty *Nails*, some whereof were *Board-Nails*, above three Inches and a Quarter long.

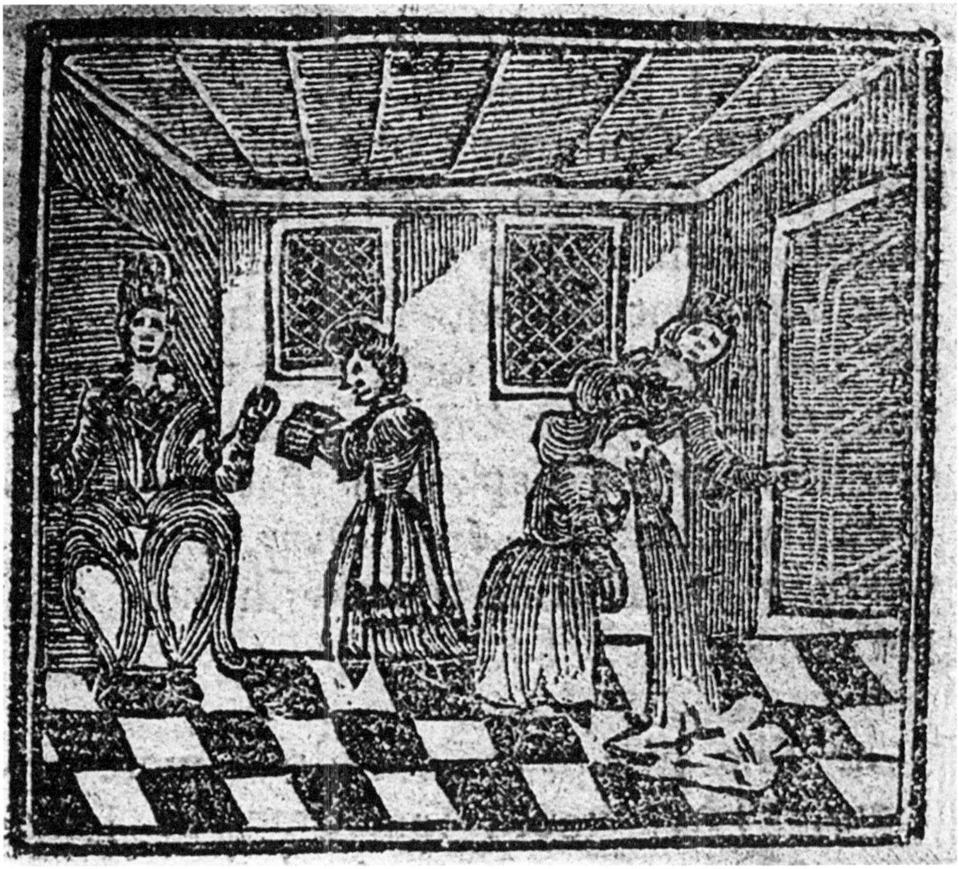

The bewitchment of Mary Hill.

Mary Hill is also readily identifiable in the Beckington registers. Her parents were John and Mary Hill and she was baptised on 16 April 1671. Once again the accounts are absolutely correct – she was, indeed, eighteen at the time of her bewitchment in 1689. Mary and Elizabeth Carrier were closely acquainted, the latter probably housed in the village poorhouse that still stands at the west end of Goose Street. Just as the 'witch' conformed to stereotype, so did the bewitched – young and vulnerable, a recently orphaned teenage girl living off the parish with younger siblings to support. Close scrutiny of the parish records also reveals some fascinating details of Carrier's life. It seems she had a very particular reputation in the village, one that made her an especially frightening figure in the eyes of the young: she laid out the dead. This is evident in the secondary register kept for recording, in line with a recent Act of Parliament, the affidavits sworn, typically, by the person who dressed the corpse, that the deceased was to be buried in woollen cloth. The winding of the corpse in its burial shroud was an unpleasant duty often undertaken by a poor woman in the community; sometimes it might be done by a neighbour. In 1686 Beckington suffered a devastating typhus epidemic and time after time the person recorded as swearing the affidavit that the deceased was buried in wool is Elizabeth

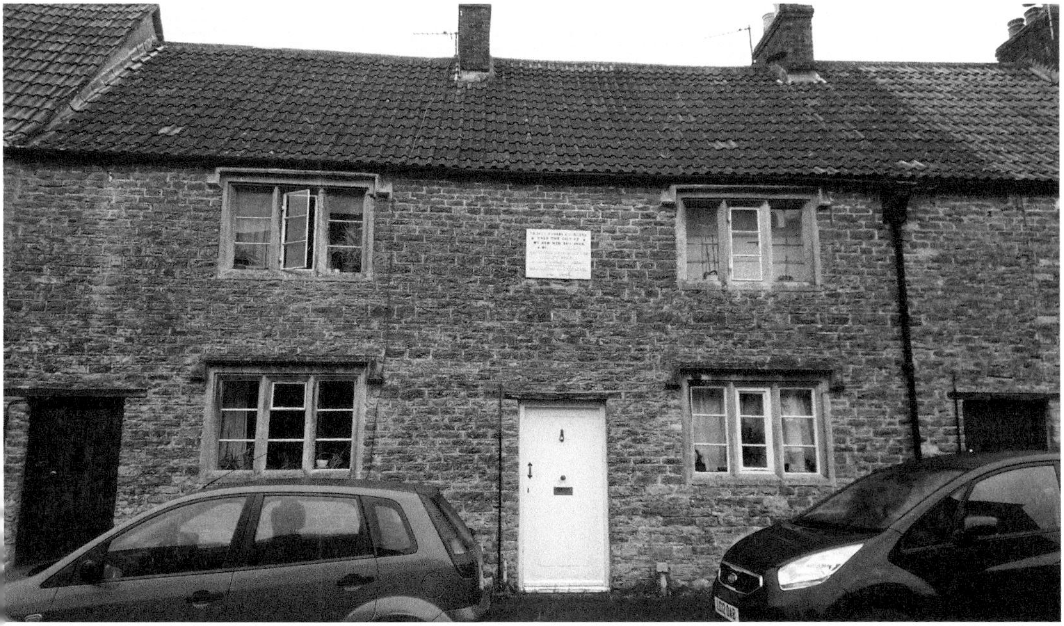

Goose Street poorhouse, Beckington. (Gary Kearley)

Carrier. In the period between September 1684 and October 1686 her name appears in sixty-one separate entries. Between the start of April and the end of September 1686 she provided forty-two of the 100 affidavits recorded, one of which was for William Spicer's father. Twelve of the fourteen listed for August were attributed to her, and in the closing weeks of the epidemic she was the only person fulfilling this role.

With the whole community rising up against her, Carrier was subjected to three 'swimmings' in the River Frome and she must have been an exceptionally doughty octogenarian to have survived. This horrible ordeal was not considered part of the due process of English law and hence, we can assume, most cases of its application were not recorded. Records of at least twenty-six cases of witch swimming in England survive for the period 1612 to 1795, the majority of which postdate the 1660s. May Hill made no reference to the swimming tests of Carrier in the account he delivered to Baxter but in *Great News* her ordeal was described in considerable detail: 'her Legs being tied, she was put in, and tho' she did endeavour to the uttermost (by her Hands), to get her self under, yet she could not, but would lie upon her Back, and did Swim like a piece of Cork.' To prove her guilt 'there was put into the Water, a Lusty young Woman, who sunk immediately, and had been drown'd, had it not been for the help that was at hand.' Most of the people watching, 200 or more, including many 'Persons of Quality', were convinced.

Having survived her swimmings, orders were given to have Elizabeth Carrier of Beckington searched for 'Marks and Tokens of a Witch' and she was committed to the county gaol at Ilchester following a hearing at the local Bruton sessions. It is highly likely that John Hunt, the son of Robert, whose book of examinations had so inspired Joseph Glanvill, was the presiding magistrate. Soon afterwards charges were brought

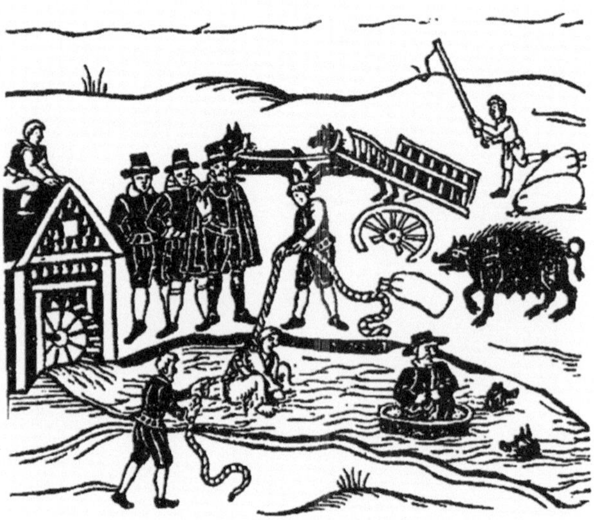

The swimming of a witch.

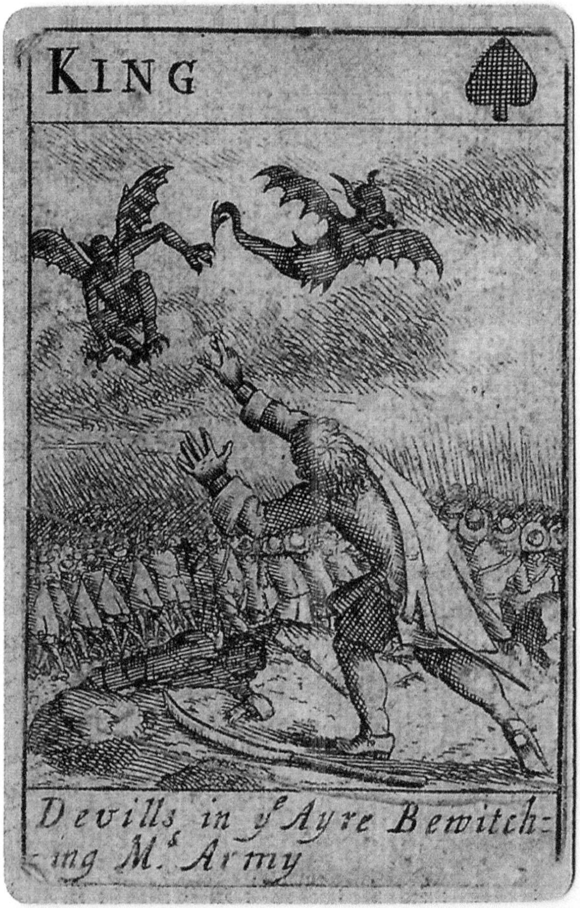

Devils bewitching the Duke of Monmouth's army at the battle of Sedgemoor, a week after his visit to Frome in 1685 (contemporary playing card).

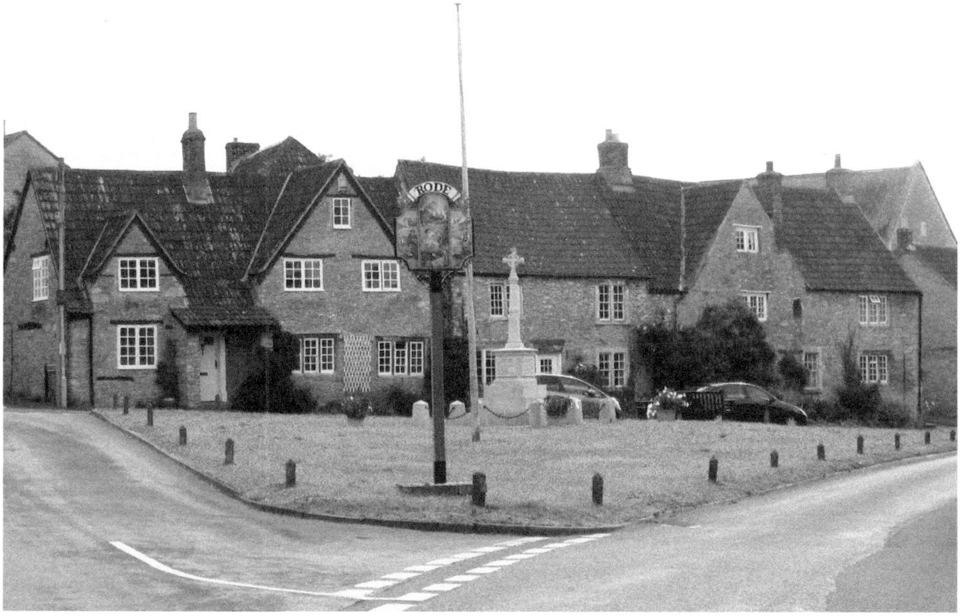

Rode, Somerset. (Andrew Pickering)

against Ann More and Margery Coombes, her alleged accomplices in the village, and they too were sent to Ilchester to await trial at the next Western Circuit assizes. Before their case could be heard, and thrown out, by Justice Holt at Taunton in April 1690, Margery Coombes died in the notoriously unhealthy confines of Ilchester Gaol – another forgotten victim in the later history of England's witch hunts.

It is unlikely to be a pure coincidence that not long after, in July 1694, a mob at Rode, another Frome Hundred parish adjoining Beckington, subjected three more women to the swimming test. Led by Daniel Keepen, a broadweaver, William Moore, a tailor, Thomas Caninge, a chandler, and William Carter, a pedlar, they broke into the house of Thomas Haberfield's mother, Anne, and took her down to the river 'and there putt her in to ye same water and continued her for a quarter of an houre until such tyme she was neere dead'. An Anne Haberfield, widow, was buried in Rode on Christmas Day 1706 – probably the same old woman who was almost drowned twelve years before. The mob also attacked Anthony Waddom when he was milking his cows with his mother on Rode Common. They 'threw down the milke of 2 Cowes and forcibly had away his mother, Margaret Waddom, to a river about 2 furlongs from ye common and there put her into ye water to see if she could swym and kept her in until she was almost dead'. When her son attempted to intervene 'William Palmer fell on him and beat him and tore a good coat from his back.'

When the men from Rode arrived at Elizabeth Kneall's elderly mother's home, they commanded her daughter to open the door so that they could take away 'ye old Witch'. Moore, who seems to have been the ringleader, instructed Palmer to break down the door and the mob entered the house. Next, preventing her daughter and son 'with a great deal of Violence' from intervening, they 'seized their mother and pulled her out of the house and had her away to a River in Rode and there putt her into the water'. Her son managed to free himself and save her from drowning but, after he got her safely on the bank, the old woman's assailants threw her back in again and kept her there 'till such tyme she was almost dead'. Elizabeth Kneall also complained in her testimony that William Moore had stolen a knife she kept 'in her bosome', perhaps for self-protection from such as he. Meanwhile, one Oswald Browne was accused of being a wizard and threatened with a swimming 'as they had don three old women before, and also threatened him [that] if he did nott come forth then they would have him and his wife out ye next day or else they would fyre his house about his Eares'.

A similar episode occurred in Frome in 1730, shortly before the repeal of the 1604 Jacobean witchcraft act in 1736. The case, first reported in the *Daily Journal*, appeared four months later in the first edition of the long-running *Gentleman's Magazine* in January 1731 under the title 'The Melancholy Effects of Credulity in Witchcraft'. This related how the supposed bewitching of a child of one Wheeler, seized with strange unaccountable fits, led to a poor old woman in the neighbourhood being dragged out of her home and carried on a saddle around 2 miles to a millpond. Here she was stripped of her upper clothes, her legs were tied, and, with a rope about her middle, she was thrown in. A riotous crowd of around 200 watched as 'she swam like a cork.' Half-drowned, she was given brandy and dumped in a stable. An hour later she was dead. According to the report, 'although above forty persons assisted in the fact, [...] none of them could be persuaded to accuse his neighbour, so that they were able to charge only three of them with manslaughter'. It is said that this took place in the Woodlands district on the south side of Frome. If so the millpond in question was almost certainly the one that once supplied Goose Marsh Mill at West Woodlands, a cloth manufactory that once stood on the stream running from Maiden Bradley down to the River Frome, and a short distance to the north of Court Farm.

DID YOU KNOW?

The 'swimming' of at least five so-called witches is recorded for villages around Frome between 1689 and 1730. This was the traditional test carried out to demonstrate a witch's guilt by observing how a body of water, a pure substance, rejects evil. If she sank she was deemed innocent; if she floated she was guilty. To prevent the accused from treading water or swimming it was customary to bind a long rope around her waist held by men on each bank of the pond or river in which she was immersed.

4. Heroes and Villains

According to the *Anglo-Saxon Chronicle* King Eadred came to the throne in 946 and reigned as King of England for nine and a half years, before dropping down dead on a visit to Frome in 955. Apparently Eadred was late for his own coronation as he was in bed with both the Lady Aelgifu and her mother Aethelgifu, trying to decide which one to marry! When the Domesday Book was compiled in 1086 a great pre-Norman Conquest minister, Reinbald, was living at Frome. Reinbald had served Edward the Confessor as Chancellor of England; McGarvie has described him as 'the most important politician ever to be connected with Frome'.

During the era of the Wars of the Roses, Ankarette Twynyho was the name on everyone's lips in Frome. On 12 April 1477 the widowed Ankarette was at her Frome home, Keyford Manor, when, just after lunch, the house was surrounded by upwards of 100 men sent by Edward IV's brother, George, Duke of Clarence. George's wife Isobel had died the previous December, some two and a half months after giving birth to a boy, who himself had died in January. In his grief, George believed that his wife had been poisoned by Ankarette, who was a lady in waiting to Isobel. Ankarette was taken to Warwick, found guilty of giving the duchess a 'venomous drink of ale mixed with poison' and was executed within three hours of the verdict. She was posthumously pardoned by the king, no doubt influenced by news that several members of the jury had visited Ankarette in the brief period between sentence and execution to apologise for their guilty verdict. This was just one instance of Clarence's high-handedness which so infuriated the king, ultimately leading to his execution for treason – drowned in a barrel of malmsey wine – less than a year after his dreadful mistreatment of poor Ankarette.

Bishop Ken, whose tomb can be seen at St John's, Frome, is considered to be one of the fathers of modern English hymnody (the composition and singing of hymns). He was given the bishopric of Bath and Wells by Charles II, although his appointment had more to do with matters of the heart than religion. Ken was living in Winchester as chaplain to the bishop at the time and the king wanted Ken's house for his mistress Nell Gwynn. Ken refused to move out, so the king promoted him to get him out of the way, and had Nell installed in Ken's former home. Ken was obviously a man of principle, but his high morals got him into trouble with the new (Catholic) king, James II, when he refused to publish James' *Declaration of Indulgence*. He was immediately arrested and sent to the Tower of London on charges of 'High Misdemeanour'. He was subsequently acquitted and swore an oath of allegiance to James, but when months later William and Mary took the crown in the Glorious Revolution, Ken refused to swear allegiance to the new king, declaring he could not so long as the old king was still alive. He was removed from his post and spent the rest of his life as a house guest of Lord Weymouth at Longleat, where it is said he named the viewpoint on the ridge above the house 'Heaven's Gate'. He had left

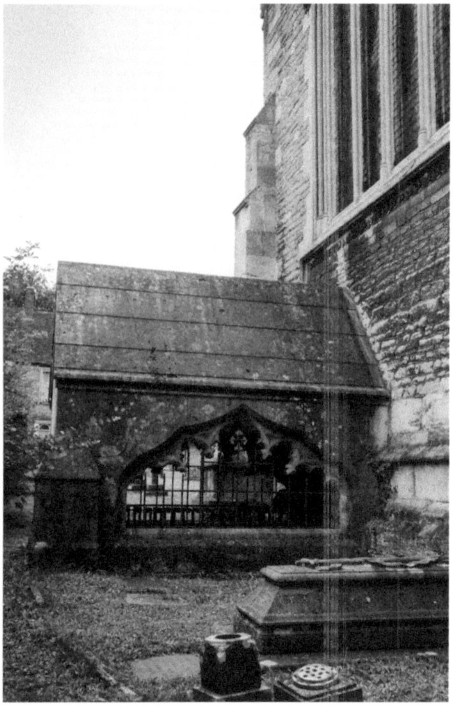

Bishop Ken's tomb at the rear of St John's Church. (Martin Kearley)

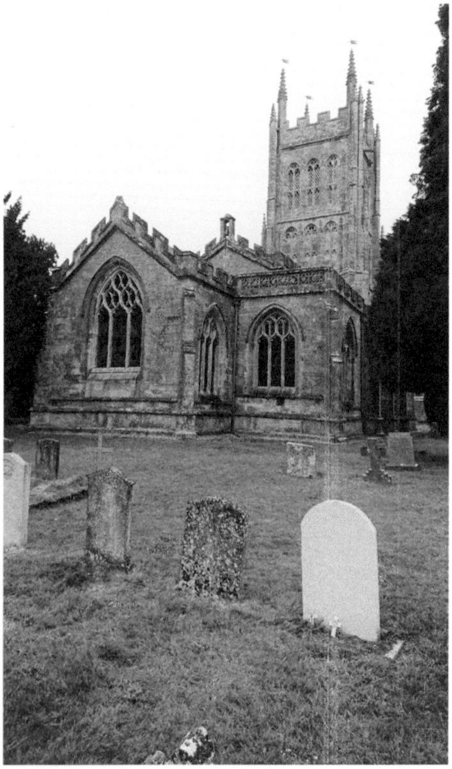

St Andrew's Church, Mells. (Gary Kearley)

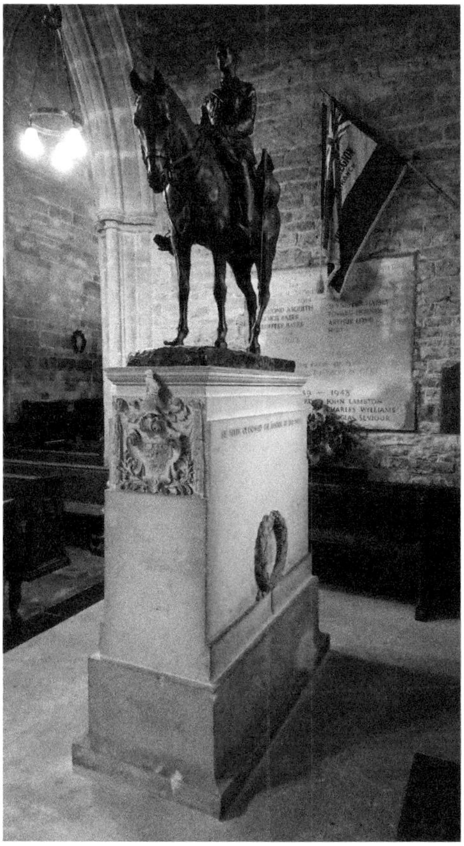

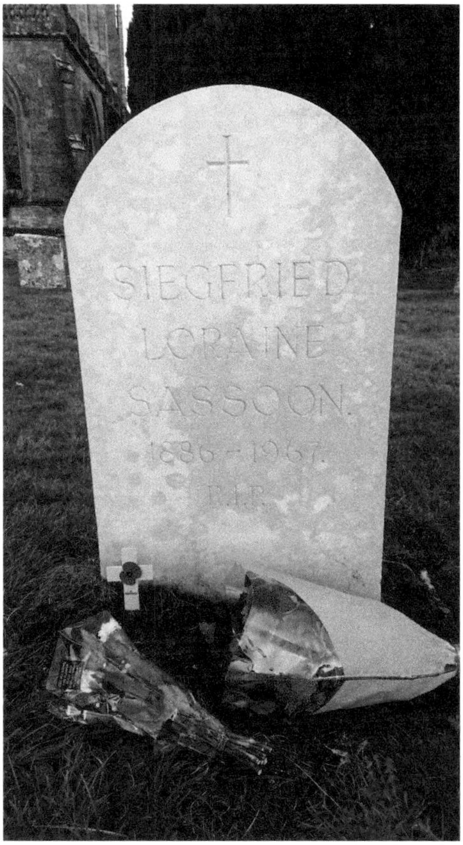

Above left: Memorial to Edward Horner in Mells Church. (Gary Kearley)

Above right: Siegfried Sassoon's grave, Mells. (Gary Kearley)

instructions that when he died he should be buried in the nearest parish church within his old diocese and this is how he ended up in Frome churchyard in 1711. Ken's standing is underlined by the fact that he attended both the deathbed of Charles II and the execution of Charles' son James, Duke of Monmouth.

The Horner family of Mells is associated in folkloric tradition with Jack Horner of the famous nursery rhyme; the plum he pulled out of his pie considered by some an allusion to the transfer of the Mells estate to John Horner following the dissolution of Glastonbury Abbey. A remarkable life-size bronze statue of a First World War army officer astride his horse can be seen in St Andrew's Church in the village. It was sculpted by the well-known painter of equestrian scenes Sir Alfred Munnings, and commemorates the life and untimely death of Edward Horner, who was killed at Cambrai on the Western Front in 1917. In the churchyard, among other eminent individuals, can be found the grave of the First World War poet Siegfried Sassoon.

The daughter of Somerset wool merchant Walter Singer, Elizabeth Rowe was born in 1674 and, in around 1690, moved with her family to Frome where she met and married

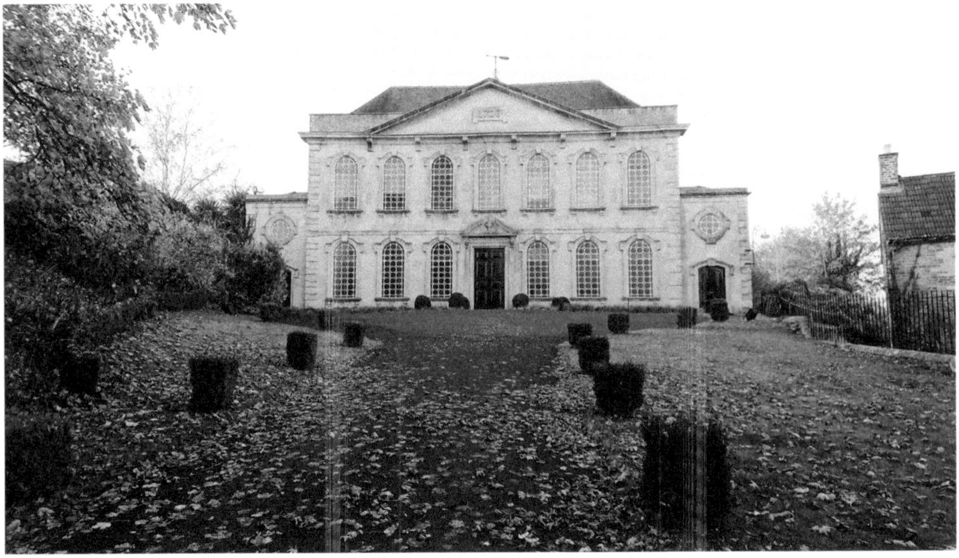

Rook Lane Chapel, built in 1707 for nonconformist worship. (Gary Kearley)

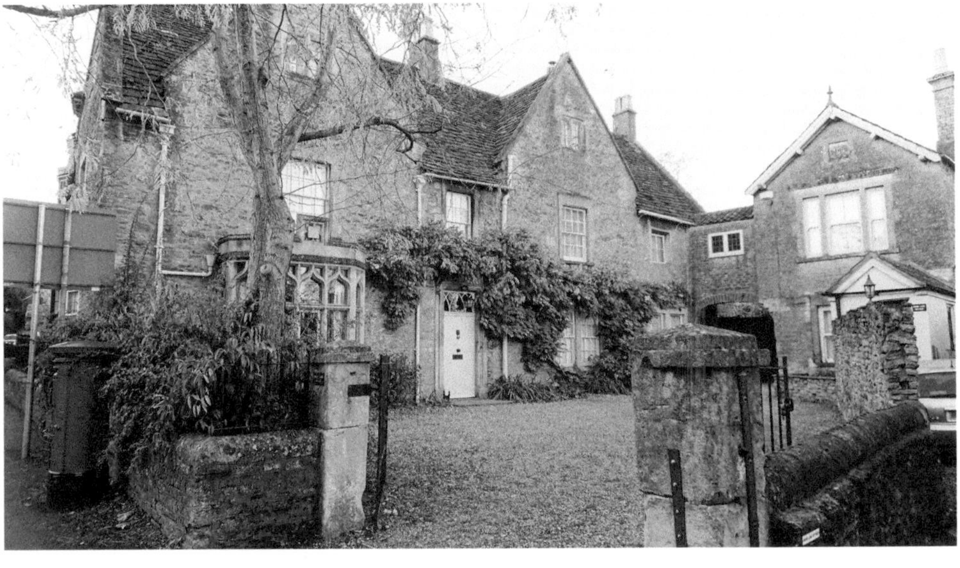

Rook Lane House, Elizabeth Rowe's Frome home. (Gary Kearley)

Thomas Rowe in 1710. After her husband's death she lived in Rook Lane House until her own death in 1737 and she is buried at Rook Lane Chapel. Rowe, little known today, established a considerable reputation for herself in the eighteenth century as a writer of religiously inspired poetry and other devotional literature.

Rowe's contemporary, the leading-light of the Methodist movement, John Wesley, preached in the town on many occasions. This remarkable evangelist who, after receiving

Holy Orders at Oxford, spent two years as a minister in America at Savannah, Georgia, before returning to Britain to spend most of the rest of his long life as an itinerant preacher, enduring the discomforts of endless tours on horseback to bring his message to tens of thousands of his ardent followers, particularly people in manufacturing and mining communities. He left an extensive record of his travels in his journals and letters. His novel approach to his ministry, considered radical, even dangerous, by his opponents, frequently provoked a hostile reaction when he arrived in town. During one of his many visits to Frome at the site of what became Christ Church, a mob seeking to break up an open-air meeting in Pack Horse Fields pelted him with mud and rubbish that included the rotting corpse of a cat. In addition to making at least nineteen trips to Frome, Wesley also preached at Mells and, on three occasions, at Rode.

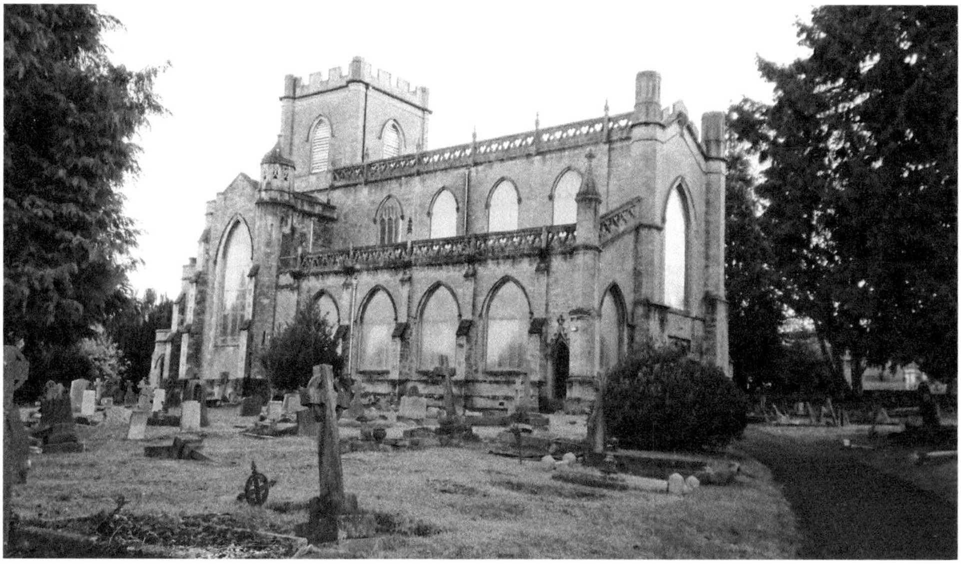

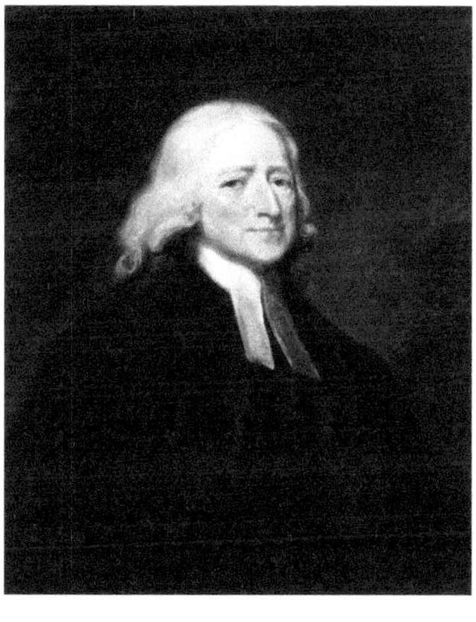

Above: Christ Church, built in 1818 on Behind Town (later renamed Christchurch Street West). (Gary Kearley)

Right: John Wesley.

At the start of the eighteenth century Daniel Defoe remarked that Frome was reckoned more populous than Bath and by the end of that century it had a population of around 9,000. Hunger riots in Frome in 1737 and at Beckington in 1766, resulting in a handful of deaths, were indicative of the precarious lives of ordinary folk throughout this period of industrial progress.

In 1773 Richard Smith and ten other men were brought before magistrate Thomas Horner for assaulting John Harebottle. The accused were said to have hoisted poor Mr Harebottle onto a pole and then carried him through the streets of Frome, blowing a horn. What had Harebottle done to deserve this? In his defence Smith claims that Harebottle had made 'attempts of a detestable nature' against him while walking home from the pub. Smith had told his work colleagues and they had decided to take matters into their own hands. The magistrate dismissed the case due to the heinousness of Harebottle's behaviour.

DID YOU KNOW?
John Webb Singer started out in brassworking as a maker of altar candlesticks in 1848. He made his moulds out of turnips. The war memorial that stands outside the Memorial Theatre in Christchurch Street West was cast in 1922 by Singer's. It is modelled on Charlie Robbins, an employee of Singer's who fought in the First World War.

The Reverend W. J. E. Bennett is the man responsible for the current appearance of St John's Church. Hounded out of St Paul's in Knightsbridge by his parishioners for his Catholic leanings, his friend the Marchioness of Bath secured him the job at Frome. He soon set about restoring/ruining the church (depending on one's view) remodelling it largely with his own funds. It was thought to have cost him £40,000, well over a million in today's money. The work undertaken was controversial both then and now, with many features reflecting his interest in the Anglo-Catholic Oxford Movement. One obvious manifestation is the magnificent Via Crusis, thought to be unique in an English parish church. In 1852, writing to her husband, the famous philosopher Thomas Carlyle, Jane Carlyle concluded 'Frome is a dull dirty-looking place, full of plumbers: one could fancy that the Bennett controversy must have been a godsend to it.' Prime Minister Benjamin Disraeli, on the other hand, considered the restored St John's 'marvellous, exquisitely beautiful and in admirable taste'.

Frome has long had a reputation for innovation in industry and was the birthplace of several noted engineers. Benjamin Baker (later knighted) was born on Butts Hill in 1840, and his birth is celebrated with a plaque on the wall of the fire station. He is best known for designing the Forth Rail Bridge (voted Scotland's greatest man-made wonder and now a UNESCO World Heritage site) and the first Aswan Dam in Egypt. He also helped build the Metropolitan and Northern Underground Lines in London. Cleopatra's Needle was

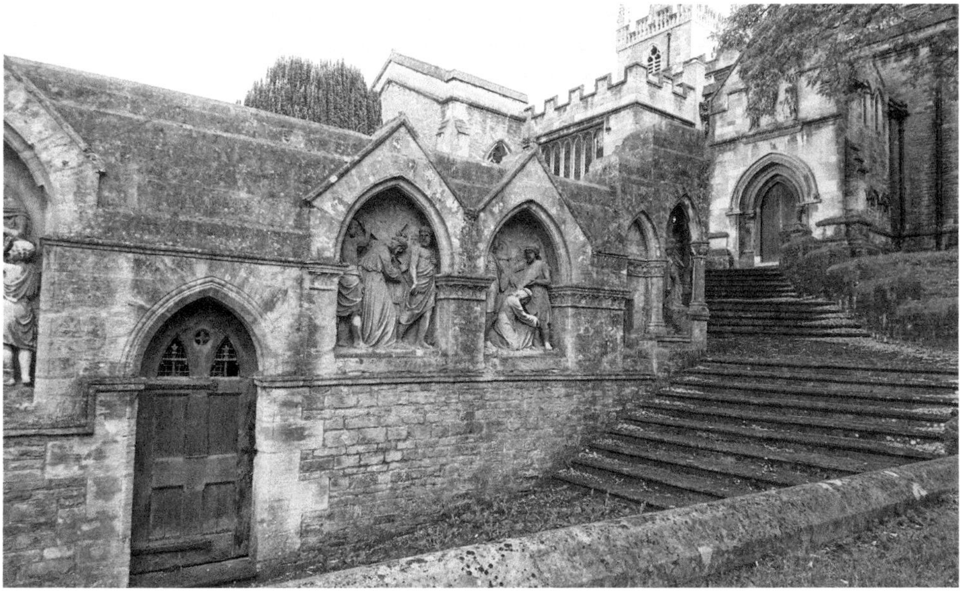

St John's unique Via Crucis. (Gary Kearley)

brought from Egypt to London in a purpose-built ship designed by Baker. The statue of Boudicca in her chariot near Westminster Bridge in London and the statue of Justice that stands proudly atop the Old Bailey near Blackfriars Bridge were both designed and cast in Frome by Singer's, the foremost art foundry in late nineteenth-century England. The statue of Alfred the Great in Winchester and the famous Capetown lions were also cast in Frome. Singer's engineers were established by local man John Webb Singer in 1854, whose first casting efforts were toy cannons as a schoolboy. World famous for its statues, the firm started out making 'medieval' candlesticks and other neo-Gothic metalwork for churches. The company was taken over by TYCO, which now manufactures water sprinklers on Marston Trading Estate.

The year 2017 finally saw flowing water return to the Boyle Cross in the Market Place. The cross was given to the town by Reverend and Mrs Boyle of Marston House in 1871. Thomas Bunn, the man responsible for so many improvements in the town, had tried to install a fountain some years earlier, but the heavy vase he erected was taken away in the night, thrown into the river and smashed.

In the era when Britain was celebrated as 'the workshop of the World', iron tools of the finest quality were being produced by the Fussell family close to Frome in the vicinity of the villages of Mells and Nunney. They established six manufactories in the area, utilising the available local labour, fast-flowing streams, wood and coal. Ironworking in the Wadbury Valley at Mells had taken place for an uncertain length of time prior to the granting to James Fussell III in 1744 of permission to build a new manufactory. Here ample evidence of his and his successors' activities survives in ruinous form. The remains of furnaces, forges, railway tracks, metalled paths, sluice gates, and even a waterwheel can be found in a state of quiet dereliction in this damp wooded valley. The Fussells

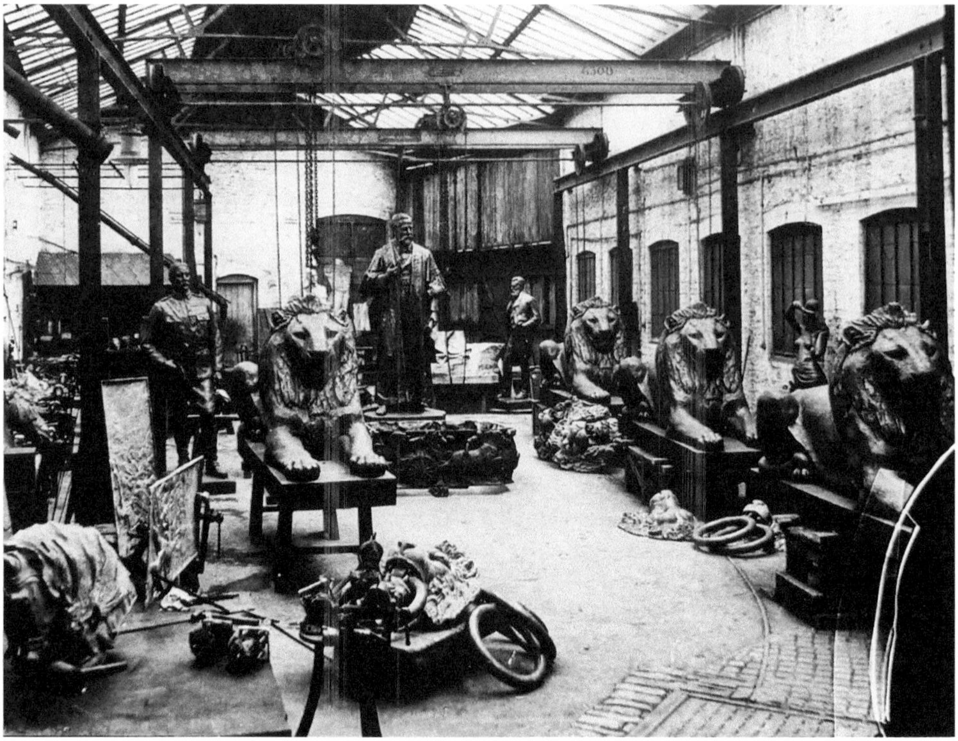

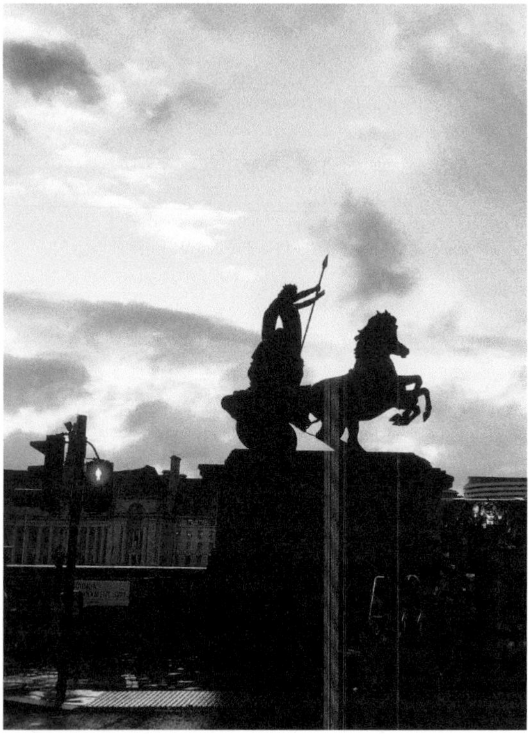

Above: Inside Singer's factory.

Left: Made in Frome: the Boudicca statue in London. (Andrew Pickering)

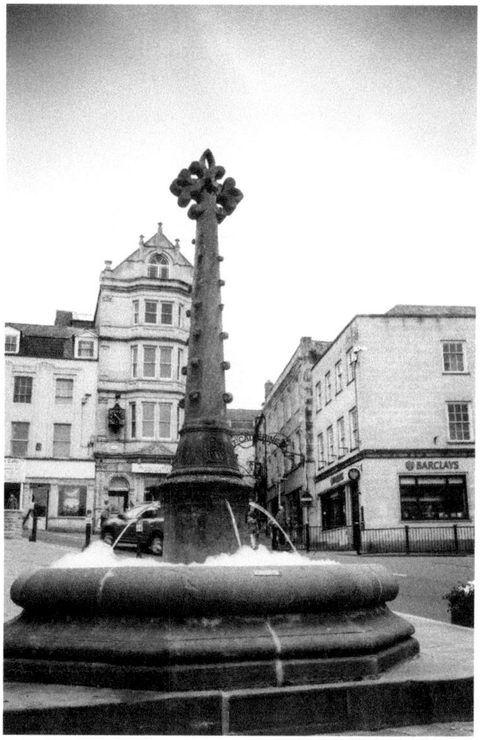

Boyle Cross with added foam – typical quirky Frome. (Martin Kearley)

were a major employer and representatives of a new entrepreneurial 'aristocracy' – lords of their own new manor at Chantry, eclipsing the longer established Horner family of neighbouring Mells. The church they built is decorated on the outside with images of angels holding reaping hooks and other tools of their trade. Their products were sold throughout Europe and also in America. At Mells they specialised in the production of improved scythes and other bladed agricultural tools. In so doing, particularly in the time- and labour-saving production of quality scythes, which increasingly replaced the shorter sickles of antiquity, they made an important contribution to the contemporary 'revolution' in agriculture. In 1803 a newspaper article acknowledged the company's contribution in the struggle to defeat Napoleon:

> At this eventful and momentous crisis, when the heart of every Briton beats high with true loyalty and patriotism, we feel pleasure in recording the spirited offers made to Government for the defence of the country. Mr James Fussell, of the Mells Iron Factory, near Frome, has offered to prepare (gratis) 1,000 pikes, and afterwards to supply the Government with 2,000 weekly as long as they may be wanted. (*Bristol Journal*, 6 August 1803)

When, in the late 1820s, Colonel Thomas Horner refused to sell the Fussells the freehold on the land beside the Wadbury stream where the Fussells had their works, the ironmasters retaliated by renting one of the few parcels of land in the village not

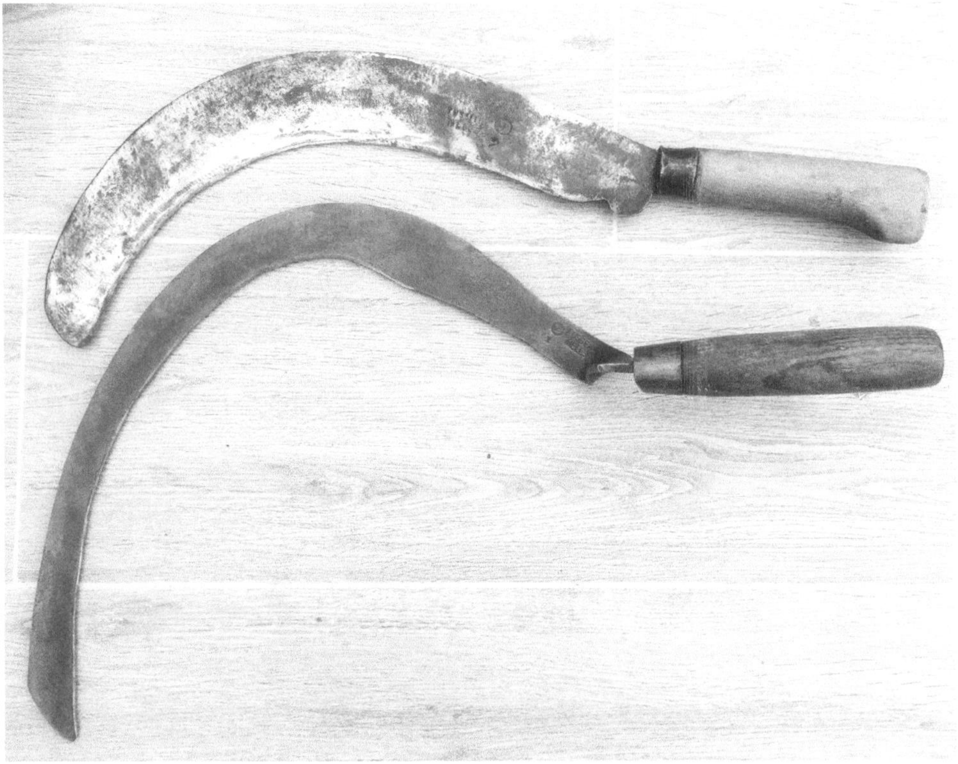

Agricultural tools made by Fussells of Mells. (Andrew Pickering)

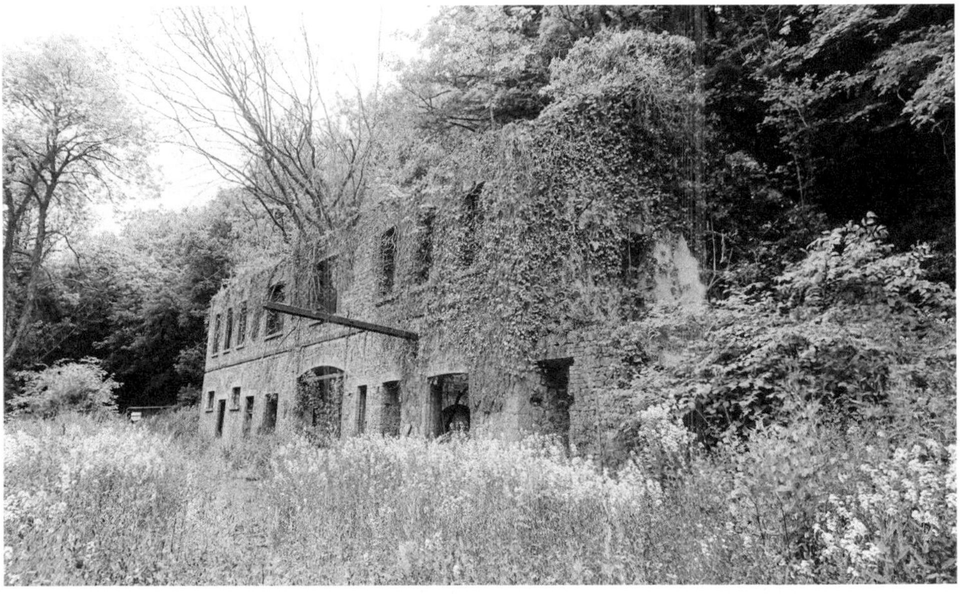

Fussell's ironworks today. Some restoration work has started. (Gary Kearley)

owned by the Horners and set about their noisy and noisome work, hitherto confined to the distant valley, on the doorstep of Mells Park House. After more than ten years of wrangling the colonel eventually conceded defeat. The new works near to his home were dismantled and, in 1841, the freehold was handed over.

At the start of the 1850s a pair of villains, William Maggs and William Sparrow, were at the heart of the criminal fraternity in Frome and were the first names in the frame when any crime was reported. When fourteen-year-old Sarah Watts was raped and strangled at Bottle's Farm while her parents were at market, Maggs, Sparrow and their associate Robert Hurd, a prize fighter known as 'Frome Bob', were suspected. They were charged with the murder but acquitted for there was no compelling evidence and all had alibis. Maggs and Sparrow were soon back in trouble, accused this time of cheating their cow-owning neighbours in night-time milking raids! Before they could be arrested they were spotted breaking into Thomas Bunn's property. They evaded capture, leaving behind a cheese stolen earlier from Plaister's grocers, and went on the run. A search of Maggs' house found large quantities of stolen goods in spite of Mrs Maggs' efforts to keep the constables at bay by threatening them with a loaded gun. The two felons were soon picked up by the authorities and each sentenced to fifteen years transportation to Australia for the milk theft. Maggs broke out of prison but was swiftly recaptured and sentenced to deportation for life for stealing the cheese. In 1852 Sparrow's sentence was increased from fifteen years to twenty-five for his part in the cheese theft. He also managed to escape from prison, but he too was recaptured, and both made the long voyage down under. Sarah Watts' murderer was never identified.

DID YOU KNOW?
The statues of a young boy and old woman decorating the front of the Blue House are those of Billy Ball and Nancy Guy, created by a stonemason named William Langley. They proclaim the original dual use of the building as a school for twenty boys and housing for twenty elderly women. Conversely Keyford Asylum, long since demolished, provided accommodation for twenty young girls, in training for service, and twenty old men.

The sorry tale of Constance Kent of Rode was retold to considerable acclaim in Kate Summerscale's *The Suspicions of Mr Wicher* (2008) and has been the subject of several books, TV documentaries and films. She eventually confessed, in 1865, to the murder of her three-year-old stepbrother, Francis Savill Kent, whose body was found stuffed in the outside privy of the family home, Rode Hill House, in 1860. He had been taken from his cot at night and his throat was deeply cut, almost to the point of decapitation. The lack of blood at the scene suggested post-mortem mutilation following suffocation. Constance was sixteen years old when she, allegedly, killed him. Her death sentence at Salisbury Assizes was commuted to twenty years in the penitentiary at Portland. In later life, having

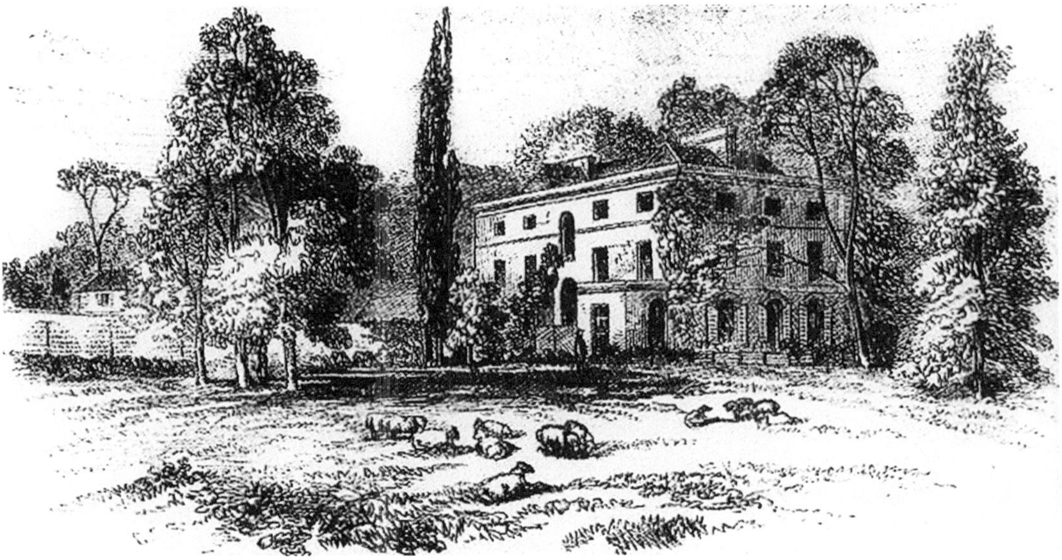

Rode Hill House, scene of a grisly murder.

changed her name to Ruth Emilie Kaye, she worked for many years as a nurse in Australia. In 1944 she received a telegram from the king, George IV, in recognition of her 100tth birthday. The Scotland Yard inspector in the enquiry, Jack Wicher, is thought to have provided inspiration for the fictional detective in Wilkie Collins' *The Moonstone* (1868).

An equally horrible murder of a child was reported in the *Bath Chronicle* in January 1766. The previous December a weaver, William Whelpley, of Oldford near Frome, struck his apprentice, 'a Girl of about Seven Years of Age', so violently with some kind of club 'that he fractured her Skull' and she died shortly afterwards. He was found guilty of 'Wilful Murder' and, at the time of the report, he was incarcerated in the county gaol at Ilchester. A few years earlier, in 1763, the same newspaper reported the sorry fate of a miller from Great Elm who hanged himself 'having been detected in Sodomitical Practices'. As was customary in such cases, his body was buried in unhallowed ground at the principal crossroads in the village.

Fifty-one-year-old farmer George Britten of Woolverton secured an unenviable place in our local history as the last man to be publicly executed at Taunton. On 18 July 1867, just a few years after the murder of Francis Savill Kent in neighbouring Rode that had attracted so much country-wide attention, he beat his wife, Martha, to death. Despite his attempt to conceal the murder by burning the body, he was soon discovered. When he was hanged on 29 August a crowd of around 200 watched him die. His body was then placed in a pit of quicklime where he was buried in the prison grounds.

This enduring fascination with untimely death is evident in another grisly tale published in the *Western Flying Post* in May 1831. When a drunken soldier, William Halford, a private of the 28th Foot, was run down and killed by the post-chaise in which he had been travelling, the villagers of Beckington flocked to the church and queued to rub their faces with the dead man's hand – a traditional cure for cysts and other ailments.

In 1924 an inquest was held in Frome concerning the mysterious death of twenty-one-year-old Robert Walter of West Forest Farm in Marston Bigot. He was found with a shotgun wound to the head and his own shotgun lying beside him. However, the obvious explanation – suicide – did not tie in with the evidence: both barrels were still loaded. In fact, he *had* killed himself but, it was concluded, without intent. It transpired that, nearby, he had rigged up a loaded rifle and trip wire to trigger it in order to deter deer from trampling his crops; somehow he had accidentally managed to trip his cunning device himself and thus ended his own life.

Another dreadful accidental shooting with fatal consequences occurred in Frome in 1880. Two brothers and a friend amused themselves at target practice using George Salmon's rifle and six cartridges he had stolen from the drill inspector of the Frome Rifle Corps at the end of a training session. Unfortunately, a ten-year-old lad, William Wells, had climbed a tree in a nearby garden in order to water a rose some distance beyond and in line with the target. He was shot in the head and killed instantly. The three men were found guilty of manslaughter but, being of good character, they were sentenced to just one month in prison.

A further horrible death by misadventure was that of Harry Noad of Rode in 1880. A butcher by trade, one morning before the break of day, on his way to market in Bath, his horse bolted and Harry's cart was overthrown. He was flung into a ditch and buried beneath the carcasses of several calves he had on board. He was discovered by a relative some time later and freed but his back was broken and he died soon after.

The Mount in Frome was the scene of a shocking double murder in 1926. A depressed, paranoid ex-serviceman and recently unemployed coachman, William Hoddinott, took his own life by cutting his throat with a razor after killing his fifty-six-year-old landlady Ellen Thorne and his seventy-two-year-old fellow lodger Isaac Bray. He had murdered them with a hatchet.

Major J. W. D. T. Wickham, a solicitor by trade, was one of Frome's most colourful characters. A patron of the arts and charities, athlete, superb horseman and 'a good boating man', he was awarded a medal by the Royal Humane Society for rescuing a drowning boy from the river. Like his father before him, also named James Wickham, he was an officer in the North Somerset Yeomanry, helping to quell riots in both Frome and Bristol. He later established the Frome Selwood Volunteer Riflemen and oversaw the construction of the Gentle Street drill hall for their use.

When the clothing industry in Frome went into decline in the early nineteenth century, the number of families claiming poor relief rocketed. In an attempt to ease the financial burden on the parish and to improve the lives of the unemployed, a series of voluntary emigrations were undertaken. A similar scheme organised by the parish of Corsley in 1830 had proved a great success and so, on 23 March 1831, eighty-five Frome residents were sent by carriage to Bristol to be put on board the ship *Airthry Castle,* bound for Montreal via Quebec. The parish paid for their transport and provided cash for their living expenses, it being estimated that this one-off cost to the parish equated to just two years of poor relief payments thus saving the parish money in the long run. This was repeated in 1832 when a further 140 left Frome for a better life in Canada but their ship was caught in ice for over two weeks and when they eventually arrived at Quebec

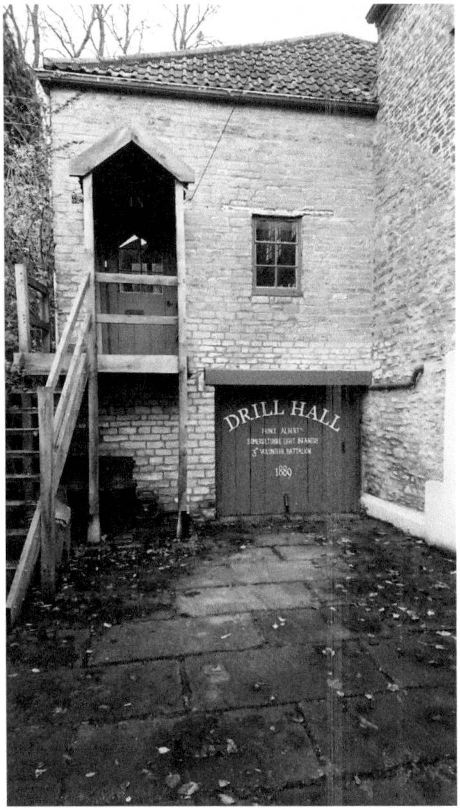

Gentle Street drill hall. (Gary Kearley)

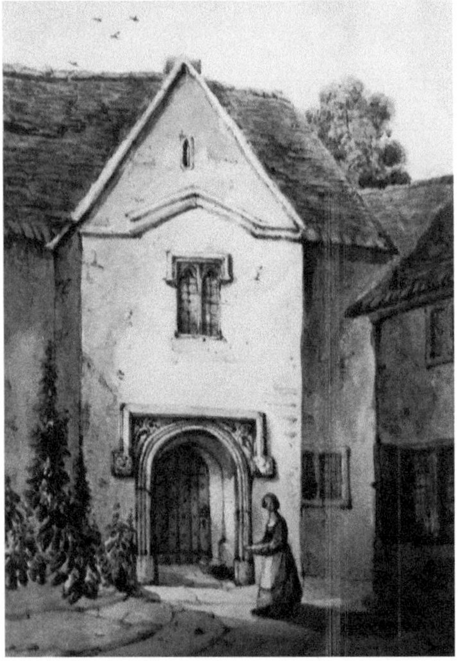

Keyford Manor, home of the unfortunate Ankarette Twynyho.

they were stranded there because someone in the shipping merchant's office in Bristol had forgotten to send the money for their onward transportation to Montreal. While awaiting this payment the emigrants were hit by cholera, which had first arrived in the country towards the end of 1831. There is no record of further emigrations taking place, although many of those who made the journey prospered in their new homes and wrote to loved ones in Frome expressing their delight with their new situation.

Frome has welcomed some important visitors over the years, including Tsar Nicholas I of Russia and a Prince of Wales (the future Edward VII). The tsar was in town one Sunday in 1844 when he stopped his coach outside the George Hotel on Market Place to enjoy a glass of sherry while travelling from Longleat House to Bath to get a train back to London. News of his presence soon spread, and the churches emptied as the crowds flocked to see one of the most famous people in the world. Edward's visit in October 1853 was much more low-key. Travelling incognito with his tutor, touring the country that he was later to rule, the twelve-year-old future king stopped for lunch at the Crown (as it was said to be quieter than the George next door). The pair must have looked decidedly travel-worn and grubby as the publican decided not to bother wasting a fresh napkin on the young prince. Edward visited again in 1881, this time bringing his wife, the future Queen Alexandra, but this visit was far from secret. Four huge sets of arches were constructed for the royal carriage to pass under, grandstands were built, and the streets were lit by 'gas devises and coloured fires' that burned all night. Edward's grandson, the future Edward VIII, visited the town in June 1923.

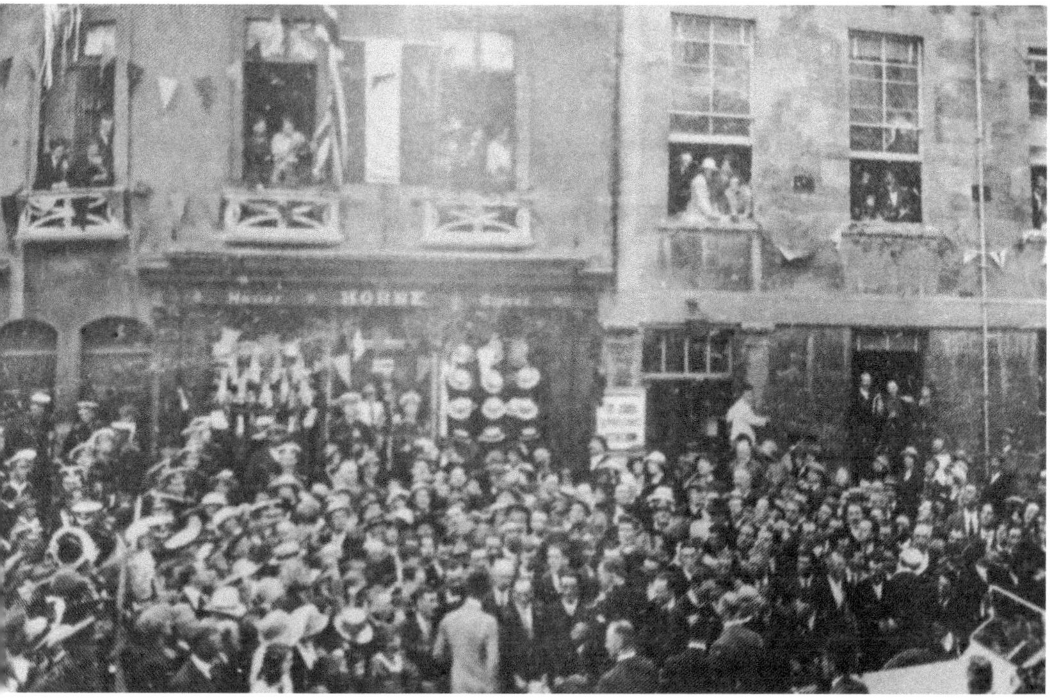

The future Edward VIII (back to camera wearing black hat) visiting Frome in 1923.

Frome contributed greatly to the war effort during the First World War, but this wasn't restricted to sending troops to fight in the trenches or raising money for equipment. In the first week of September 1917 children from the British School collected 80 lbs of conkers, increasing to 2 cwt the next week and 14 cwt during October. Conkers were a cheap source of starch to be used in the manufacture of cordite, used as a propellant for bullets and shells.

DID YOU KNOW?
Frome's tradition of holding an annual fair can be traced back as far as 1270 when a royal grant permitted a three-day fair to be held each September. The modern Frome Show, 'an Annual Cheese Show and Fair on an extended scale', was inaugurated by Robert Porteous, steward to the Earl of Cork and Orrery in the 1870s.

Following the retreat from the beaches of Dunkirk in 1940 the 3rd Infantry Division (part of the British Expeditionary Force) moved its headquarters to Frome. Major General Bernard Law Montgomery ('Monty') took up residence in the Portway Hotel on 3 June and started planning a return to France, even though the retreat from the Dunkirk beaches meant that the British Army had only enough equipment for one division. Winston Churchill and Eisenhower were both reported to have visited the town to confer with him. It is thought that officers in charge of Montgomery's security were aware of the existence of tunnels under the town and decided to utilise them as a possible escape route should the need arise. Workmen clearing the site of the former Singer's works near the current Cheese and Grain car park discovered a subterranean chamber that had five tunnels leading into it. They noticed that while four were stone lined, the one that led off in the direction of the Portway had been upgraded with a concrete lining.

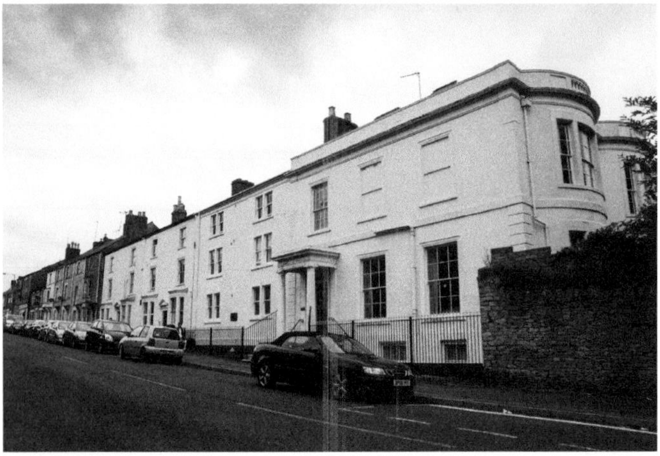

Portway Hotel, Montgomery's headquarters in 1940. (Martin Kearley)

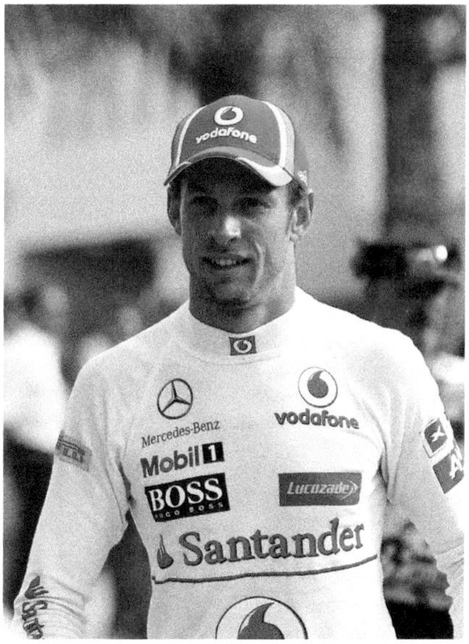

Frome's own Formula 1 star: Jenson Button. (Ryan Bayona under Creative Commons 3.0)

For many living outside the Wessex region who previously had never heard of the town, Frome has arrived on their map as the birthplace of Jenson Button, the 2009 Formula 1 world champion. Born in 1980, Button lived in Northcote Crescent on the northern edge of Frome and was educated at Vallis First School, Selwood Middle School and Frome Community College. Jenson's late father John, a renowned rallycross driver, ran a garage and go-kart tuning business called Rocket Motorsports at the top of Bath Street, opposite what is now the Cornerhouse pub. John prepared karts for his son, but Jenson was not the only customer who went on to make a name for himself in the world of motor racing: a young Lewis Hamilton, five times F1 world champion (at the time of writing) also used John's services. Jenson worked his way up through the various motor racing formulas and was clearly destined for great things but was thought to be a bit too flash when he used to collect his niece Karina from Writhlington School in a bright yellow sports car, supplied by his team. No one believed her when she boasted that her uncle was going to be a Formula 1 driver one day! When the old Bailey Bridge into the Market Yard car park was removed for safety reasons in 2010, it was replaced by a new cable stayed bridge that was named in Jenson's honour. True to Frome's green credentials, the old bridge was recycled to be used on the Wilts and Berks Canal in Melksham. As an aside, one wonders if Jenson Button is a distant relation to the wonderfully named Repentance Button who was christened in Frome in 1782.

Dave Crisp is another of Frome's modern-day heroes. Dave is the metal detectorist who discovered the fabulous 'Frome Hoard' of Roman coins and immediately reported his find to professional archaeologists, resisting the urge to dig them up by and for himself, and thus enabling the archaeologists to build a complete contextual record of the extraordinary find in situ. The excavated pottery jar contained over 52,503 coins, the second largest Roman coin hoard found in Britain. The hoard is one of the star exhibits at the Museum of Somerset in Taunton. Hoards found elsewhere in the vicinity of Frome

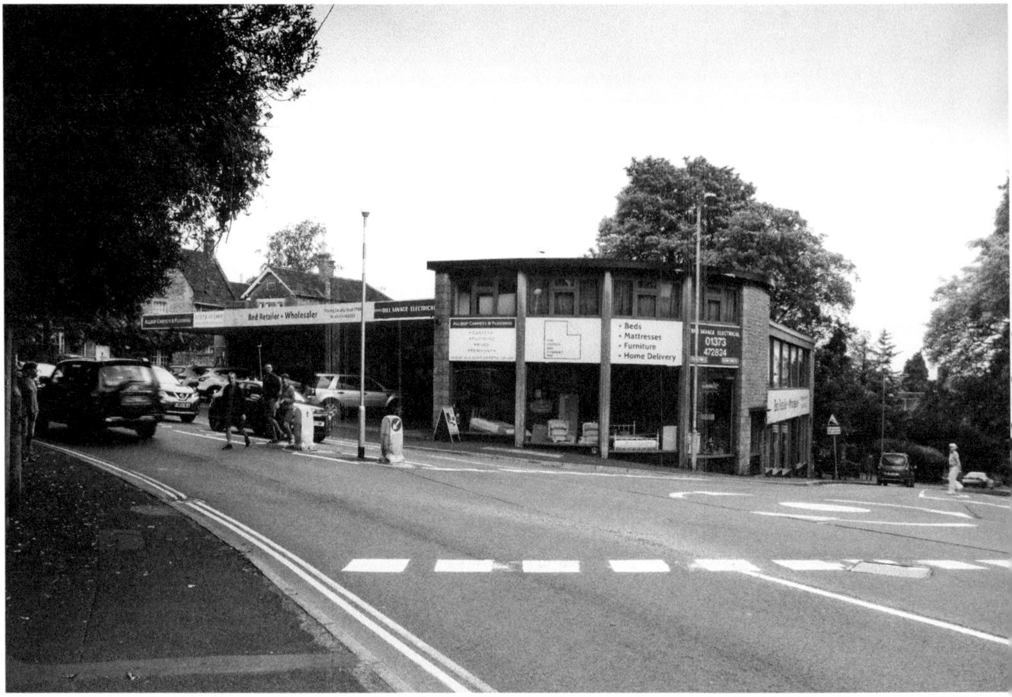

Jenson Button's father's former garage and karting shop at the top of Bath Street. (Martin Kearley)

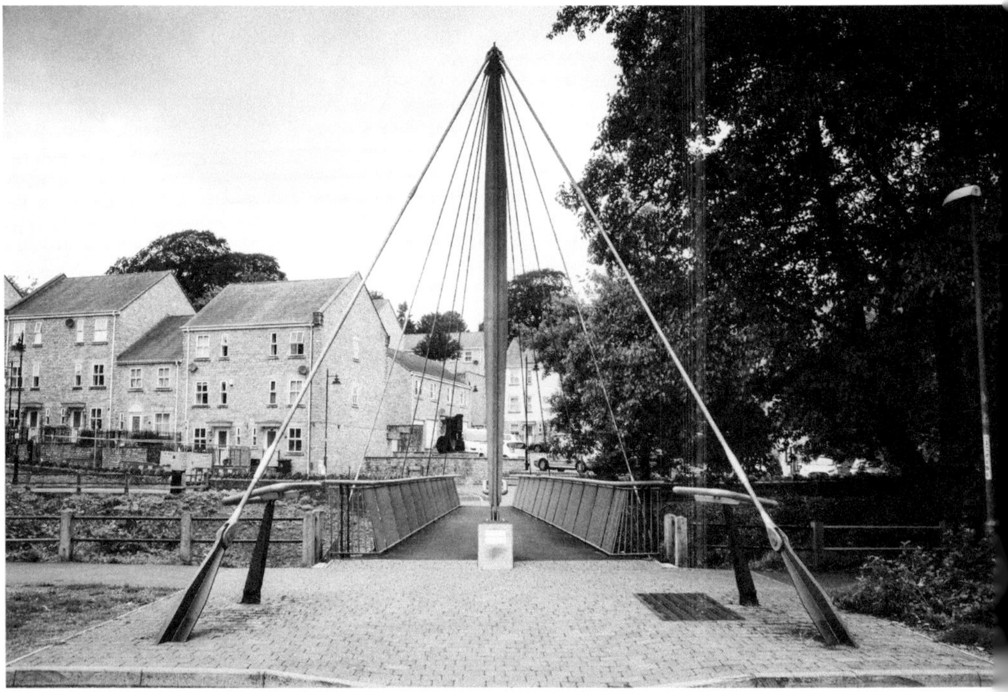

Button Bridge replaced the former Bailey Bridge. (Martin Kearley)

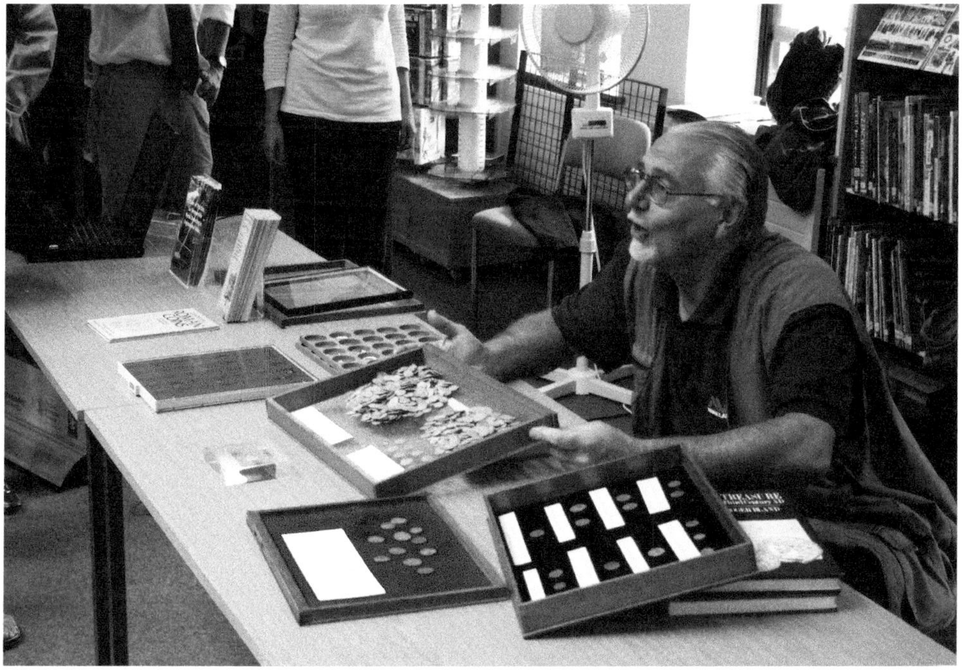

Above: Dave Crisp displays part of the Frome Hoard.

Right: The Frome Hoard in the Museum of Somerset, Taunton.

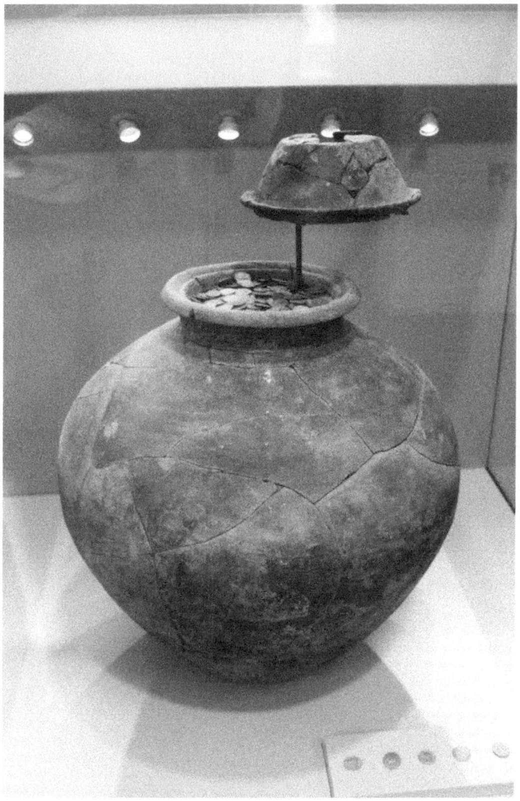

include one discovered at Nunney containing almost 250 gold, silver and brass coins. All except a Roman one dated AD 41 were late Iron Age, presumably local, British examples – indicative perhaps of the hiding of wealth at the time of the conquest in AD 43. If so those responsible never returned to recover their treasure.

If you have ever wondered why you have to take your shoes off to go through security at airports it is all down to a Brixton-based terrorist Richard Reid, sometimes known locally but erroneously as the 'Frome Shoe Bomber' for the reason that his mother, who became a focus of media attention, was living in Frome at the time of his arrest. Twenty-eight-year-old Reid was stopped when attempting to detonate a bomb on board a Miami to Paris flight in December 2001 using explosives that were hidden in his trainers. He was convicted and sentenced to three life terms plus 110 years without parole.

Numerous actors, musicians, and artists have settled in or near to Frome, some of considerable renown. The highly regarded Irish folk singer Cara Dillon lives here, as does the legendary American saxophonist Alfred 'Pee Wee' Ellis. Actor, comedian and author Charlie Higson, probably best known for writing and starring in *The Fast Show*, was born here, as was comedian and musician Richard Vranch, who regularly featured in TV comedy shows, notably *Whose Line is it Anyway*?. On the silver screen, Oscar-winning director Guy Green (*Great Expectations*, 1946) was born in the town, and Lois Maxwell, familiar to millions as Miss Moneypenny in the first fourteen James Bond movies, lived on Broadway (Broadway Frome that is!) from 1994 until moving to Australia in 2001.

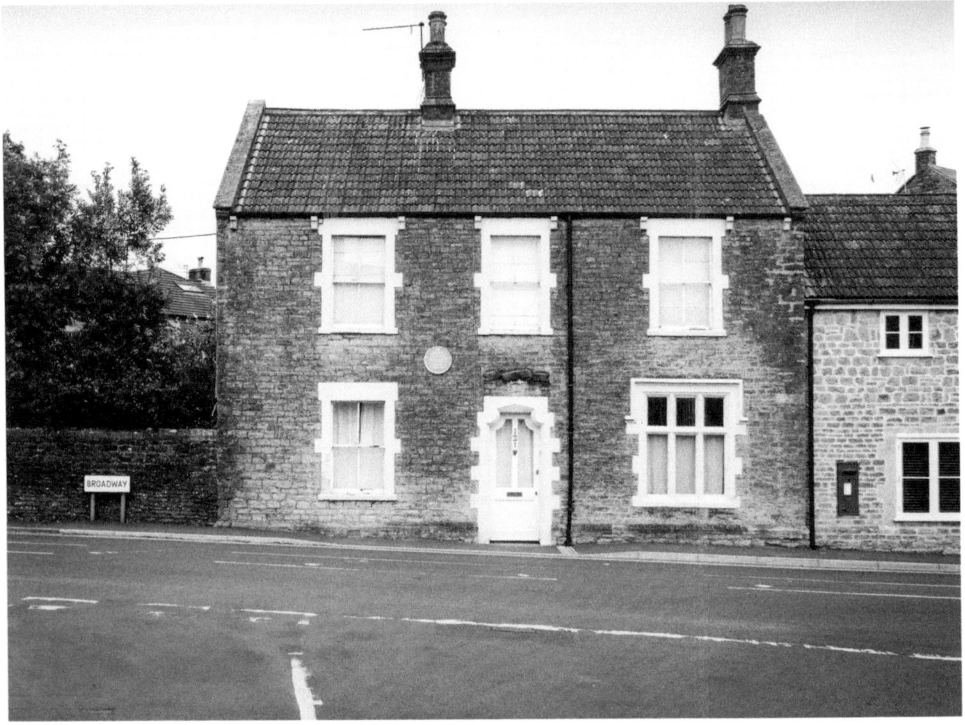

Miss Moneypenny's house on Broadway. (Martin Kearley)

5. Butts and Bartons

Evidence of ancient human activity in the vicinity of Frome has been found on occasion in the form of such finds as a heart-shaped 'cordiform' handaxe from the Lower Palaeolithic period discovered at Lime Hill Quarry near Mells. An early Neolithic gallery tomb with two side chambers, which was the last resting place of at least fifteen individuals, was razed in the early nineteenth century in the landscaping of the gardens around Fromefield House, home to the powerful clothier family the Sheppards. It could well have been of the 'Cotswold-Severn' type – similar to the spectacular West Kennet long-barrow at Avebury in Wiltshire. The remains of another massive long barrow, 85 feet long and 65 feet wide, can be seen at Rode; it goes by the evocative name of 'The Devil's Bed and Bolster'. Bronze Age round barrows are common in the region, particularly to the west of the town.

Wanstrow, on the road from Frome to Bruton, has an especially rich record of prehistoric finds: excavations between 1958 and 1961 of Tom Tivey's Hole, at the foot of a cliff at Leighton, produced Neolithic period pottery sherds, including the remains of a Windmill Hill-type cup, Roman wares, a barbed and tanged arrowhead, and a gold band thought to

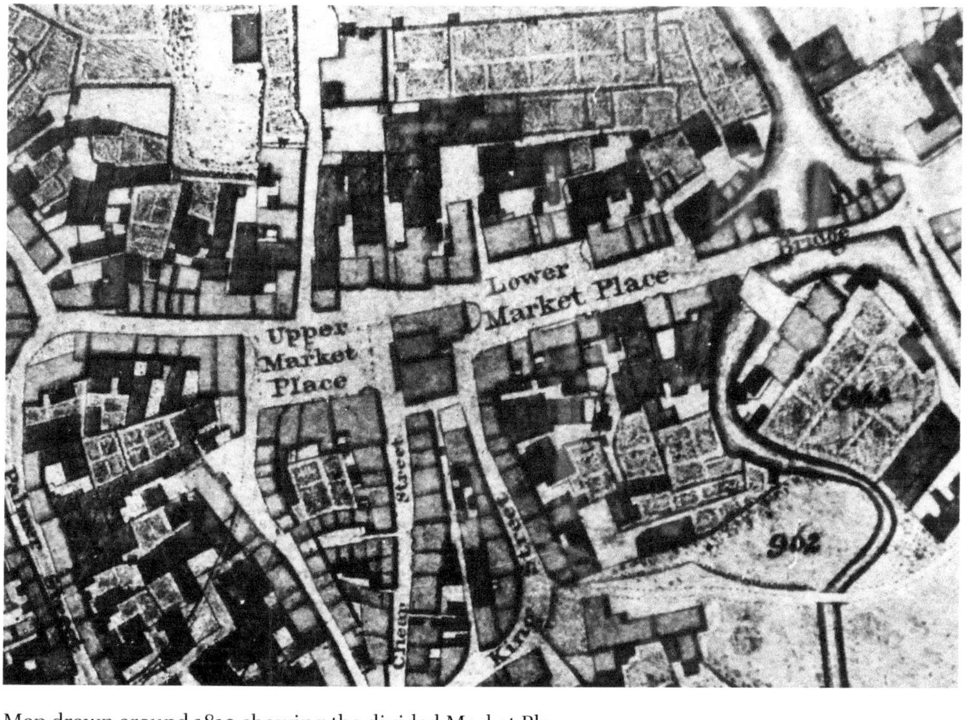

Map drawn around 1810 showing the divided Market Place.

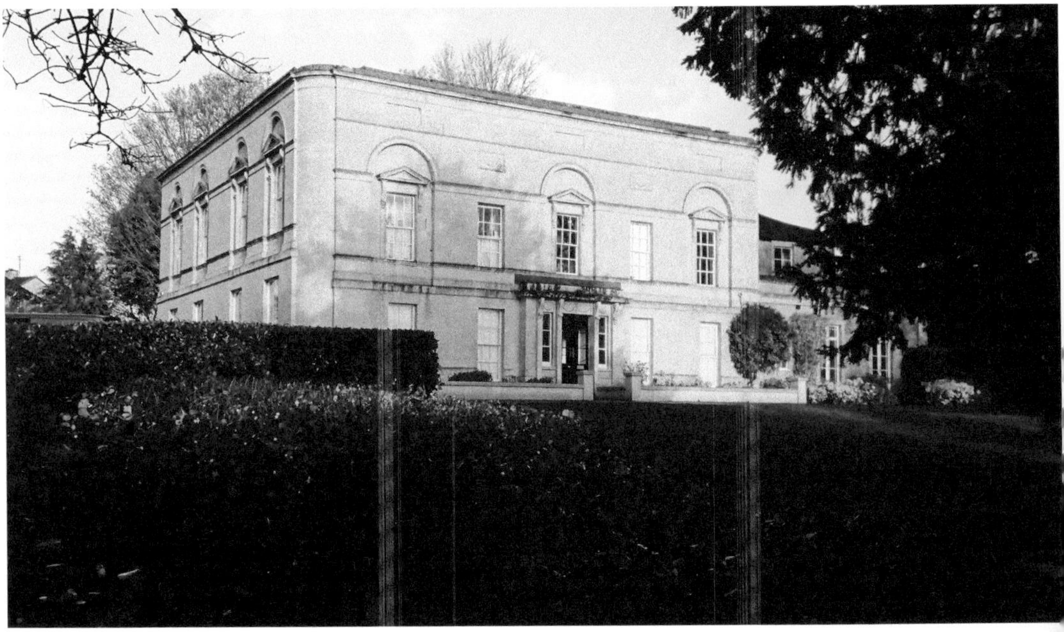

Fromefield House. (Gary Kearley)

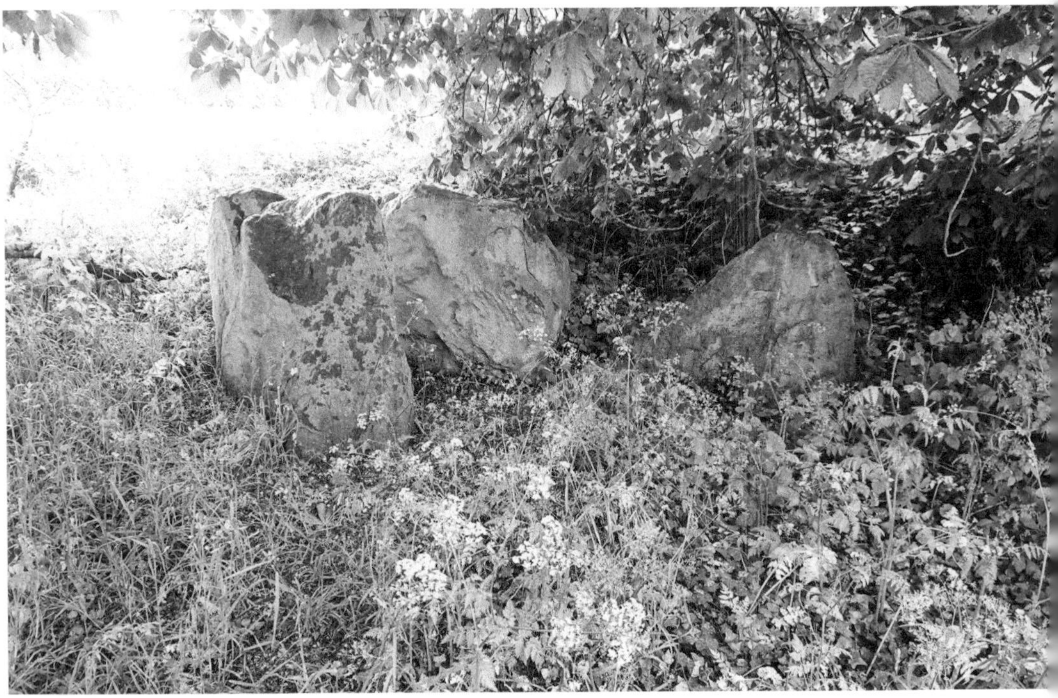

The Devil's Bed and Bolster. (Gary Kearley)

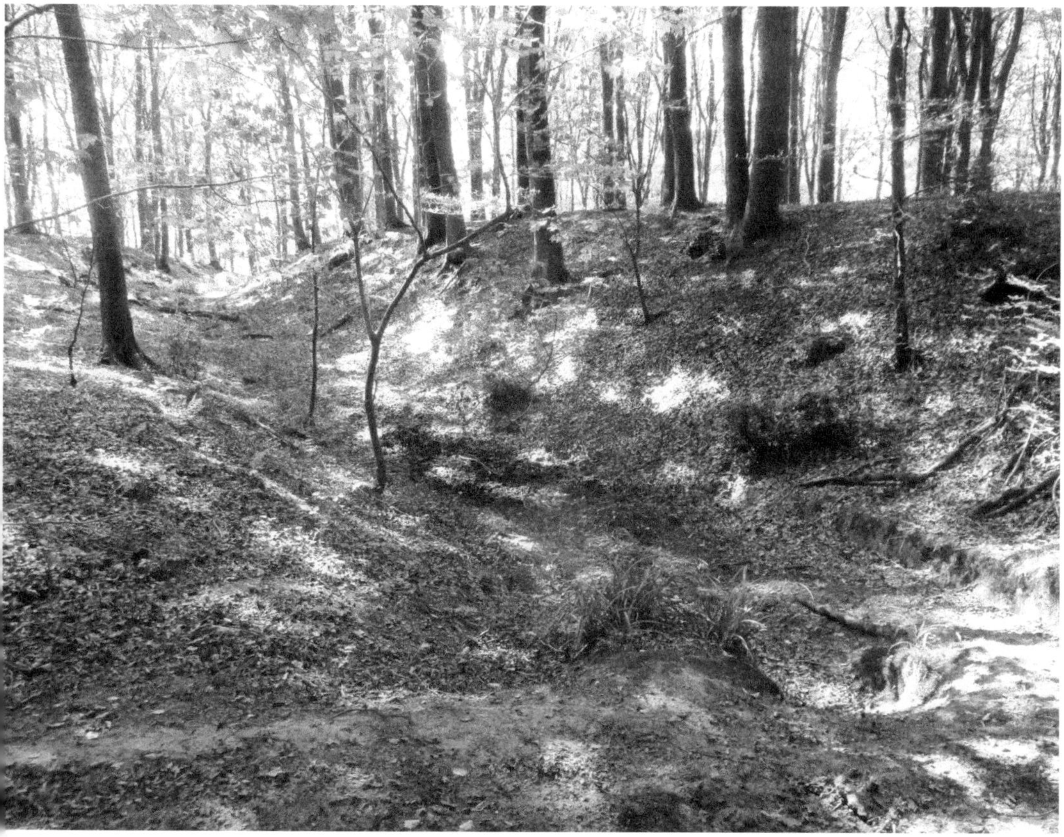

Roddenbury Camp. (Gary Kearley)

date from the Bronze Age. Tom Tivey lived very close to Frome – a Chantry man on the run who used the natural shelter as a hideaway in the nineteenth century. Animal and human bones were also found there including those, undated but considered to be Neolithic, of a forty-year-old female. The frequent '-bury' place-name suffix in the region is often indicative of early settlement activity at various hilltop locations. The remains of Iron Age enclosures and hill forts include the damaged defences of the Wadbury, Tedbury and Newbury forts in the immediate vicinity of Mells – clearly a place of considerable importance in the centuries before the arrival of Rome's legions. Hidden among beech trees and woodland undergrowth there is a large univallate (i.e. one bank and ditch) hill fort known as Roddenbury Camp on the Frome side of the Longleat estate. Even now the bank in places stands 1.6 metres high over a ditch 1.8 metres deep. Quern stones for grinding and other prehistoric tools from the locality can be seen in Frome Museum.

Romano-British era settlement is most obviously evident at the known villa sites in the region. Of these the finest local example is the Whatley villa at the edge of the parish of Nunney, found by chance in 1837. In subsequent excavations the usual paraphernalia of a very high-status Roman building, dated to around AD 300, were exposed – a hypocaust

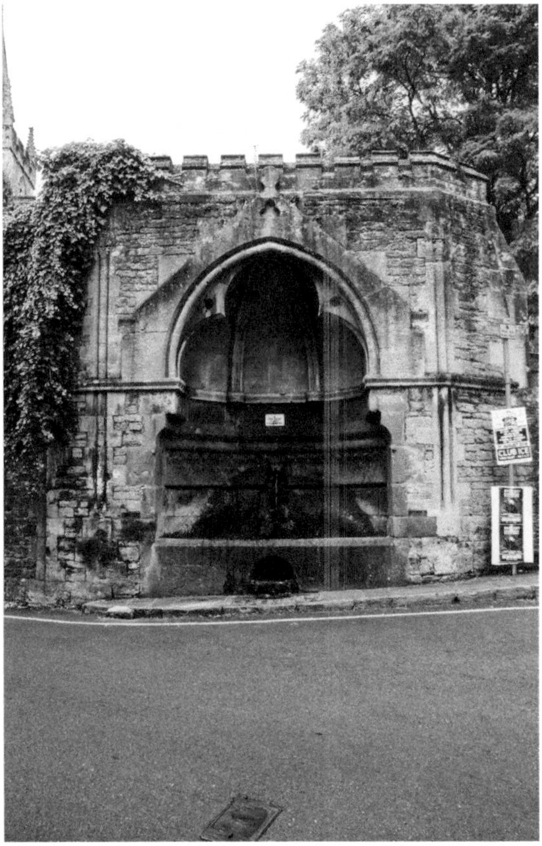

The Holy Well of Frome.
(Martin Kearley)

heating system, fine mosaic flooring, conduits for supplying water and drainage, and a bath complex.

The historic heart of Frome, and, presumably, the reason for the precise location of the original church and monastery, is its ancient spring, enshrined beside St John's as the 'Holy Well of Frome' above Cheap Street. There is a good chance this was a place of pre-Christian worship, an Iron Age shrine perhaps, predating the arrival of the Romans. Fragments of Saxon crosses have survived here, where the first church was founded by 701, and also in neighbouring Nunney.

Street names tell us a lot about the activities undertaken there in days gone by. The Butts and Butts Hill indicate that this was an area for the men of the town to undertake their obligatory archery practice, the name being first recorded in the Thynne survey of 1568. Such was the reliance on the longbow that it was the law that all able-bodied men should practice at least once a week. The last battle on English soil in which the bow was the principal weapon was Flodden in 1513 but a statute was passed in 1541 confirming that 'The Inhabitants of every Town 'shall cut Butts and shoot at them'. Despite the fact that gunpowder was taking over from the bow, Frome resident William Hackett was a stickler for the rules as he presented evidence against both Richard Style and Thomas Haberfielde in 1628, and against John Draper and Philipp Allen in 1630, for 'playing at unlawful games'

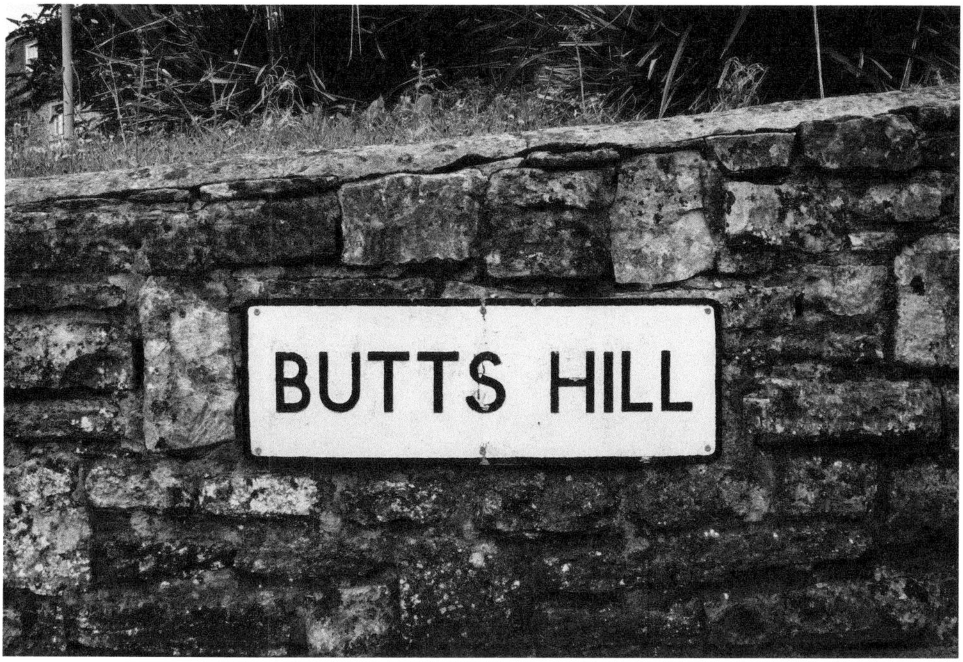

Butts Hill, an area used for archery practice in Tudor times. (Martin Kearley)

in alluding to their firing of handguns which was still, technically, banned. This archaic law was not fully repealed until 1863. Street names are not always what they seem though. There was never a castle in Castle Street; apparently it was named after a Mrs Castle who lived in what is now 'The Keep' in the 1730s. Gorehedge, despite popular notions that it denotes a place of execution or the display of the body parts of traitors captured after the battle of Sedgemoor in 1685, derives from an Old English term meaning a triangle – perhaps formed by a convergence of roads. Its earliest known appearance is in a will dated 1487. However, by coincidence, it is next to the very place (where the town's fire station now stands) where the remains of those in Monmouth's army who were hanged, drawn and quartered were displayed.

Frome, like nearby Bruton, has several 'bartons'. These days in Bruton the term denotes long narrow alleyways leading off its High Street whereas in Frome they can be short and wide, forming cottage-lined courts as is the case with Sheppards Barton off Catherine Street. The term is an ancient one and one that commemorates the agricultural origins of these places; it combines the Saxon 'bere' ('barley') and 'ton' (farmstead). Bruton's bartons, now enclosed, once led to open garden allotments beside its medieval dwellings, and the small courts of Frome's bartons perhaps still delineate the outline of ancient farmyards.

Many of Frome's street names have remained unchanged for years while others have gone through several changes. Blindhouse Lane was so named in 1798 after the town's lock-up was moved there. It had been known as Rolvestret in 1392 but was shown as Clavey's Barton on the map of 1774. When the Reverend Bennett was appointed to St John's Church in 1852 he disliked the name Blindhouse Lane and moved for it to be

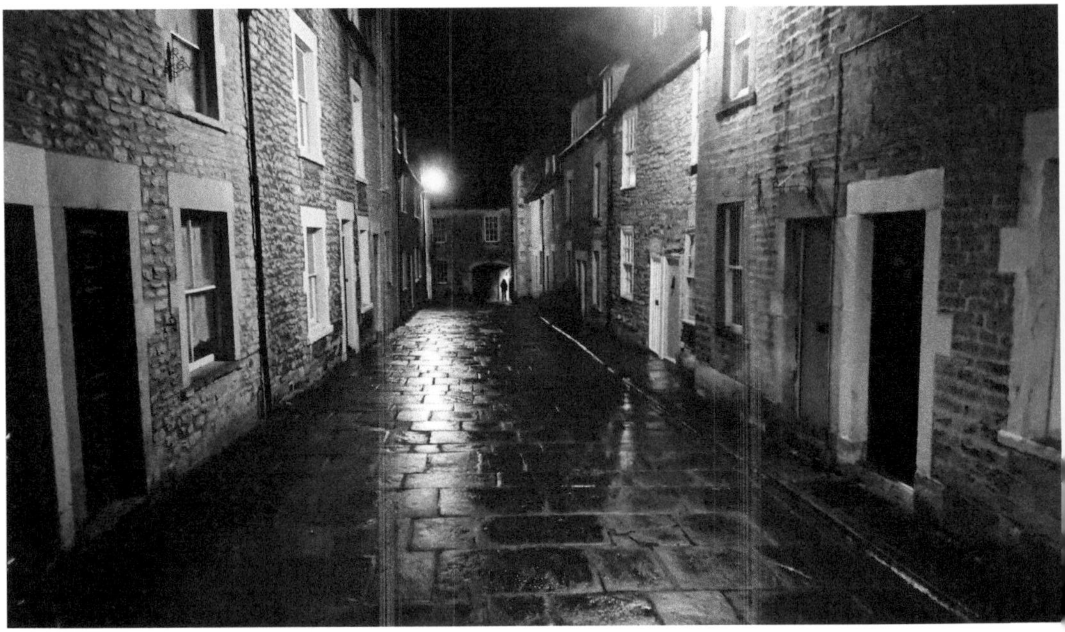

Sheppard's Barton at night. (Gary Kearley)

changed to Church Lane. It appeared in this guise on Cruse's map of 1870 and remains the official designation even to this day, although the street signs still identify it as Blindhouse Lane some 150 years after it was changed. Other places are named for the work with which they were once associated: Cut Hedges recalls hedges kept low enough to allow the wind to dry newly dyed cloth, and Rack Close implies it was a place where cloth was stretched on tenterhooks.

On the south side of Frome, 150 metres south of Tytherington, the remains of the deserted medieval village of Marston, established by 1155 at the latest, can be seen, as earthworks (a hollow way, house and garden plots, ridge and furrow features). It survived well beyond the medieval period but seems to have been obliterated for aesthetic reasons by the owners of Marston House in the eighteenth century. The site of the original manor house, the home of the Bigot family, built some time before 1195, is marked by its surviving 6-metre-wide moat.

DID YOU KNOW?

Holy Trinity Church in Trinity Street was built between 1837 and 1838. The church is in the Gothic Revival style and has a superb collection of nine stained-glass windows made by Morris & Co., designed by William Morris' close friend and Pre-Raphaelite 'brother', the famous Victorian artist Sir Edward Burne-Jones.

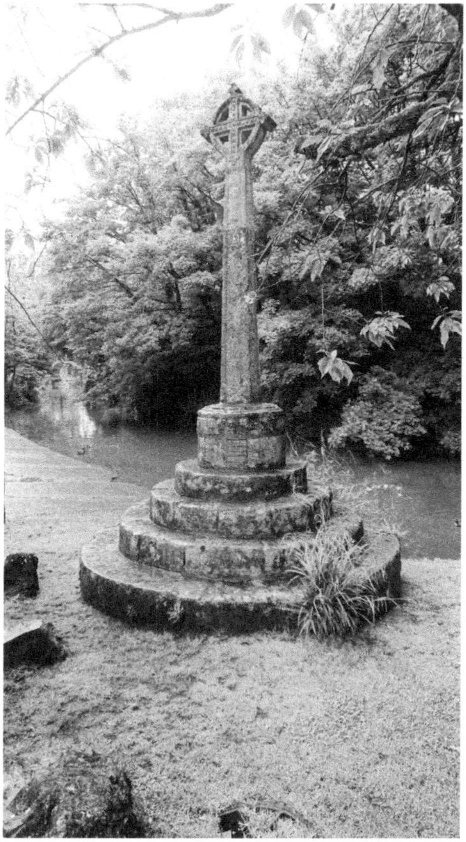

Nunney Cross. (Andrew Pickering)

3.5 miles to the south-west of Frome, Nunney is dominated by Somerset's most charming medieval castle. Said to have been modelled on the Bastille in Paris, the late fourteenth-century castle survived intact until its destruction when it was taken from the Royalists almost 300 years later in the English Civil War. The cross that can be seen raised on steps between the castle and All Saints Church once stood in the churchyard until an irate rector had it dismantled in 1869 because of the racket of children who enjoyed playing upon its stepped plinth. For almost a century it stood in a garden in the village of Whatley after a wealthy landowner there, J. H. Shore, recognised its pieces in a mason's yard and purchased them for £2. In 1959 it was returned to Mells, purchased and re-erected by popular subscription.

The monks, for whom the village of Witham Friary is named, were members of England's first Carthusian monastery, founded around 1179 in the wake of, and penance for, the murder of Thomas Becket, the Archbishop of Canterbury. The great thirteenth-century churchman (subsequently a saint) Hugh of Avalon was incumbent here for several years before becoming the Bishop of Lincoln. Only the monks' impressive dovecote, their fishponds, and the twelfth-century church for the lay brothers (friars) have survived the monastery's dissolution in 1539. As elsewhere, Frome was ravaged by the Black Death between 1348 and 1349, with probably a third or even a half of the population

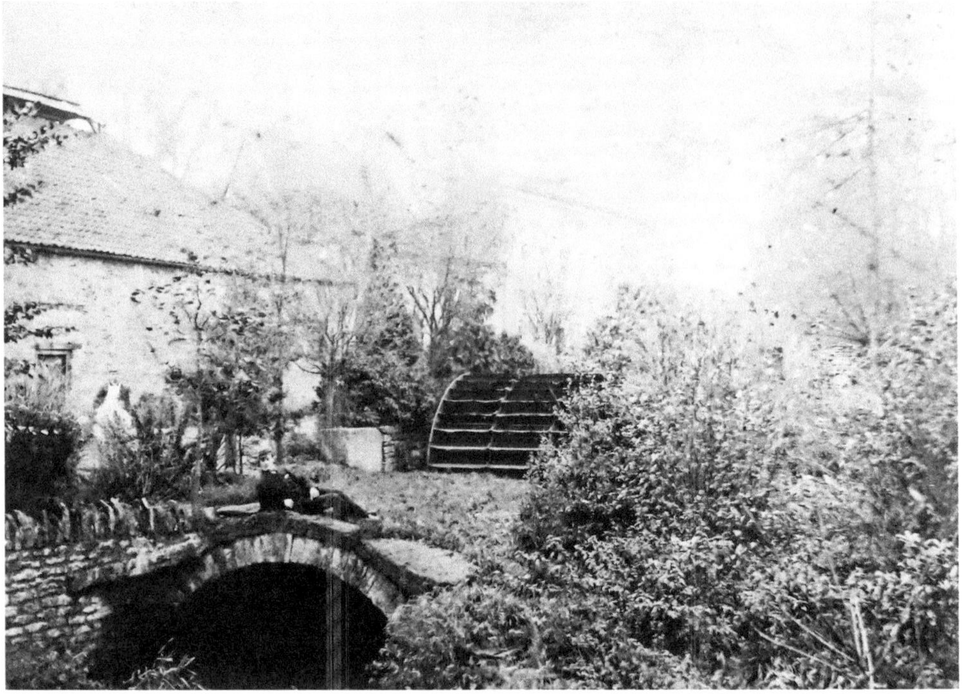

Frome Town Mill, derelict from *c.* 1850 and eventually demolished in 1960.

succumbing to the plague. Ecclesiastical records reveal that every single one of the friars perished.

In 1625 the Phillips family arrived in Frome, escaping the plague that was rampaging through London. Unfortunately, they had already contracted the disease and were placed into isolation in a house at the junction of Grove Lane and Manor Road. They lived there until the plague claimed their lives and the house, which was locally known as Plaguery House, was demolished. Despite ravaging the West Country in 1625, plague was in decline and the last epidemic in England, largely confined to London, was in 1665. However, twenty years later, from the early spring of 1685, the Frome area was again afflicted by another scourge of deadly fever. This was the most significant health scare since the Great Plague and, for a time, it looked as if it might be as catastrophic. On this occasion, thankfully, the fever did not bring plague in its wake but parish registers reveal it had a devastating impact upon many communities, including, for example, Beckington. Like the plague, it was especially severe in the summer and early autumn. It followed two years of excessive drought and hard winters; the Thames at London froze for most of the winter of 1683–84. The deleterious effect of these conditions upon public health doubtless weakened resistance to the ensuing fever. Contemporary observations suggest the fever of 1685–86 was a form of typhus, described at the time in bills of mortality as 'spotted fever'. It was recorded at the time that its 'effects were felt far more in other places' than London.

After a severe slump in the 1630s, Frome's wool trade took off, providing employment for the many and fortunes for the few. The abundance of fine townhouses and other buildings from the late seventeenth and eighteenth centuries testifies to its prosperity in this period. The nonconformist stance of several master clothiers and hundreds of ordinary folk in the town led to a remarkable proliferation of chapel building, the grandest example of which is Rook Lane Chapel. A splendid new almshouse and school complex was erected beside the town bridge in 1726 – the boys in the uniform of the Blue School added colour to the urban landscape for generations thereafter.

Built by James Pope and his team in 1707, Rook Lane Chapel is both a very early example of a nonconformist church and, architecturally, one of the finest. Following its closure in 1968 it fell prey to vandals and thieves but, after twenty-five years of neglect, it was saved from demolition after being purchased by the Somerset Building Preservation Trust and having a restoration grant awarded by English Heritage. It serves its community again as an arts centre and business premises for its present owners, NVB Architects, who refurbished and extended the Grade I listed building in 2002; appropriately enough it has also become a licensed wedding venue. The nearby Zion Congregational Church, closely associated with the Rook Lane Chapel, was built in 1810. Both churches established Sunday schools. Zion's new classroom for infants, opened in 1875, is a tiny, long forgotten, octagonal structure on Whittox Lane – its separation from the main building preventing the noise of a children's crèche from disturbing the worship of their parents. The church is now a community centre with a popular café specialising in artisan baking.

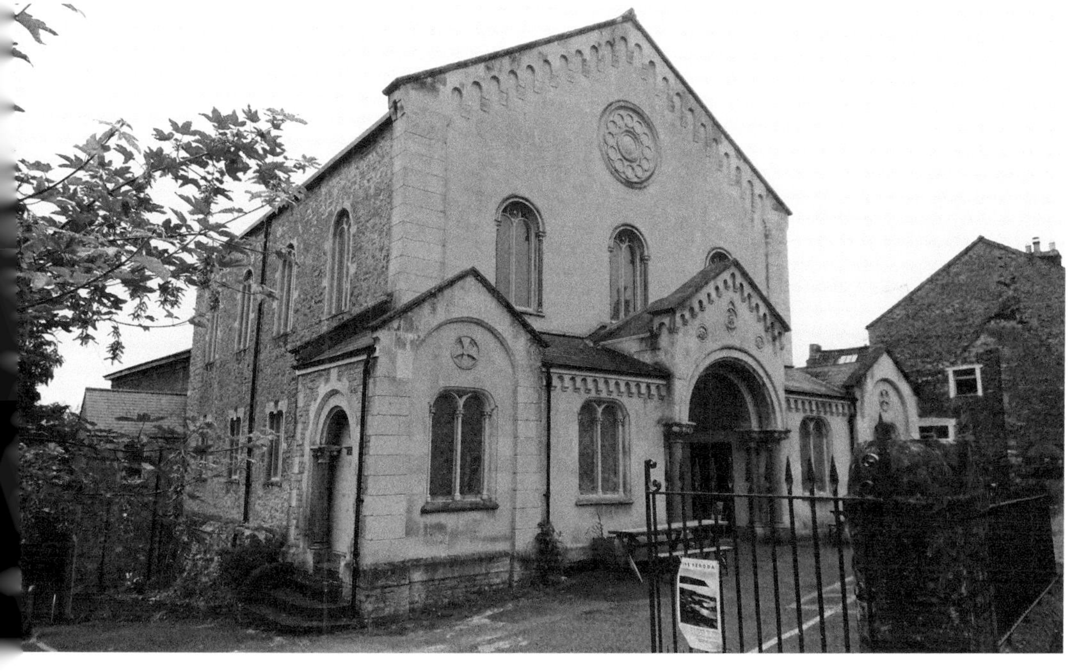

Zion Congregational Church. (Gary Kearley)

The Napoleonic Wars undermined Frome's engagement in the continental cloth trade but this, in part, was compensated for by a much-increased demand for cloth to make military uniforms. McGarvie found 800 Frome men had been enrolled in the army by 1801. Since the wars would be fought, sporadically, for another fourteen years, it can be concluded that at least a quarter of the adult male population of the town signed up – a remarkable figure that placed considerable additional burdens on the providers of relief for the poor. New machinery, loathed by the handicraft workers whose livelihoods were threatened by their introduction, helped address any shortfall in hands to produce cloth. Grim conditions in the new factories for those in work and dire poverty for those without defined the lives of thousands of Frome's inhabitants through the first half of the nineteenth century.

Until the early 1800s Frome had two market places, the Upper and the Lower, due to a large building that split the open area in two. Attached to what is now the HSBC Bank, the building was known as Phipps House, although by 1774 it had become the Crown and Thistle pub. The narrow passage from Upper to Lower Market Place was clearly impractical and the building was demolished when Bath Street was cut in around 1811.

DID YOU KNOW?
The name Vallis Vale, renowned for its rock formations, derives from the French word '*falaise*', meaning 'cliff'. Vallis first appears in the historical record in 1318 as 'Faleise'. It is famous for its geology and considered one of the best examples of rockface 'unconformity' in Britain.

The poet Henry Newbolt is buried close to Frome at Orchardleigh Park, the 'Gardenleigh' in his historical romance, *The Old Country*. The gloomy old house is not so old in fact; it was built in Elizabethan style, on the site of a much older manor house, in 1878. The small church on the island in the middle of Orchardleigh's lake, a spooky setting on a misty winter's day, underwent its own full-blown Gothic restoration in 1879. The park is also home to the remains of a Neolithic chambered tomb as well as a couple of standing stones. It is said that the tallest of these, standing a full 10 feet above ground, extends more than 10 feet below. One of the workmen who attempted to dig it up, the folklorist Ruth Tongue was informed in 1909, was killed by the falling stone, which then returned to its former upright position – one of several 'wimblestones' that can be found in Somerset.

Frome has its fair share of sports teams and clubs. These days football, cricket and rugby are among the most popular but in the eighteenth century it was back-swording that drew the big crowds. This was a form of martial art in which two men, known as 'old gamesters', would attack each other with stout ash sticks with basket handles, much like swords, in an attempt to draw blood by strikes to the head. While this was a national sport, it was generally acknowledged that some of the best players were to be found in Somerset and Wiltshire. Contests took place on an open-air stage attached to the Swan

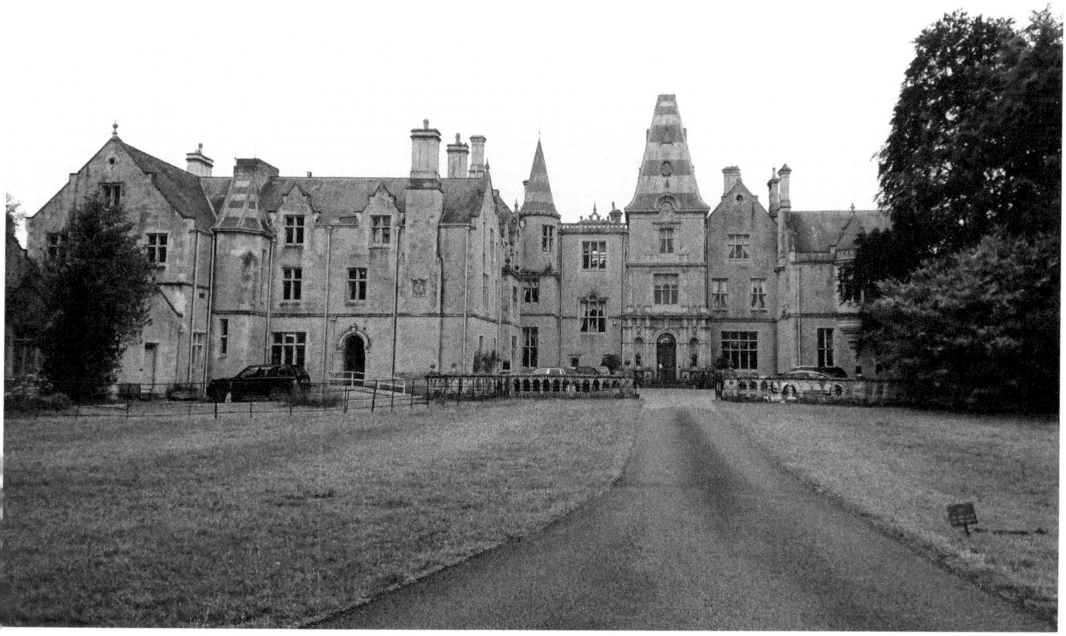

Orchardleigh House. (Gary Kearley)

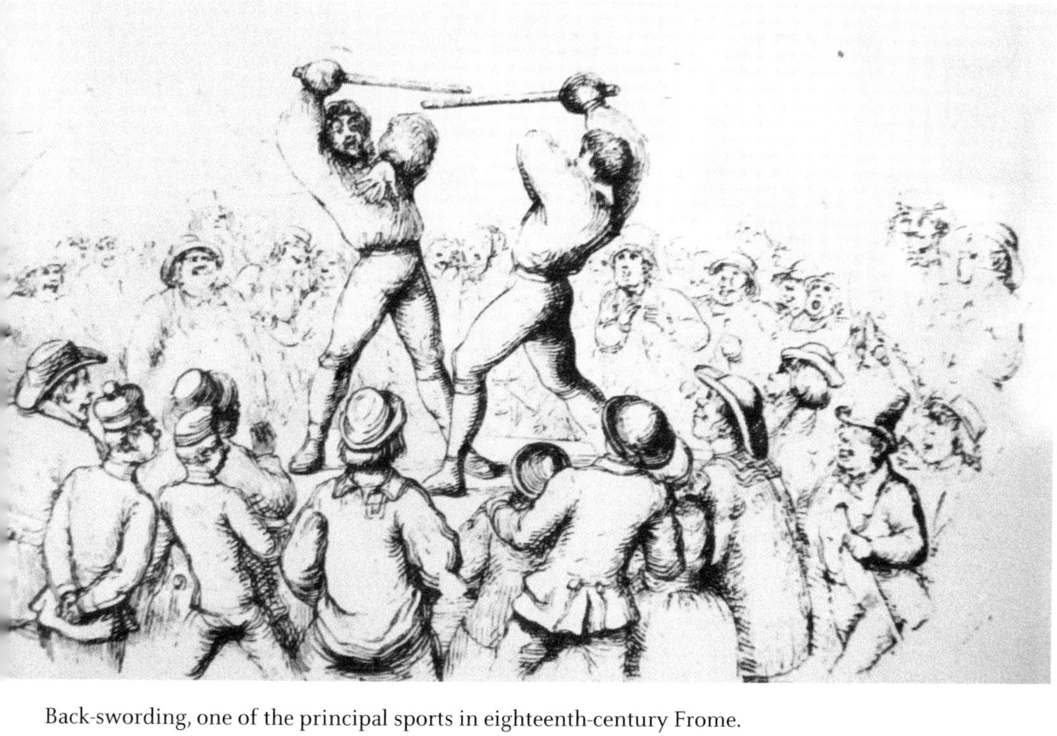

Back-swording, one of the principal sports in eighteenth-century Frome.

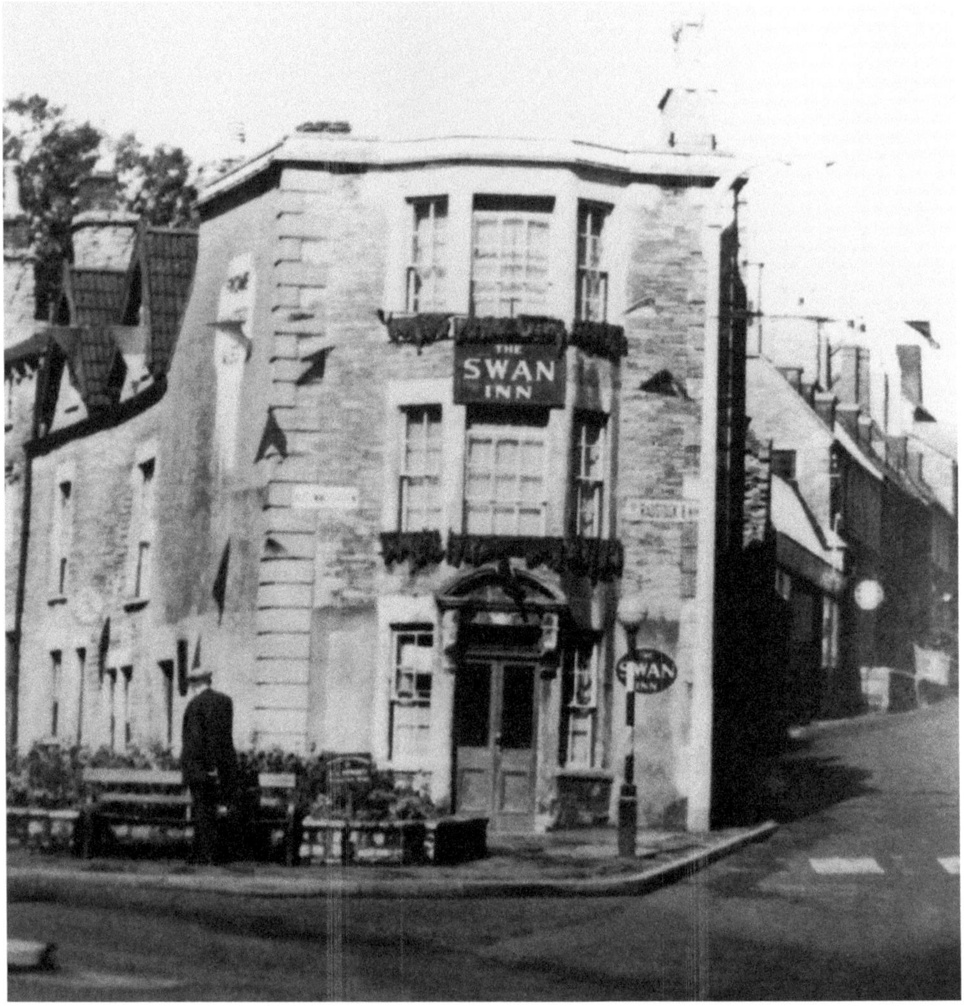

The Swan that used to stand at Badcox.

Inn at Badcox, roughly on the site of the pedestrian crossing at the junction of Vallis Road and Broadway. In 1785 *The Bath Chronicle* reported on the long-awaited clash between men from the two counties. It is reported that 'victory was declared both days in favour of the Somersetonians.' Prize money was one shilling (5p) for each time blood was drawn, with half a crown (12.5p) going to the winner of each bout.

Have you ever wondered what the odd stone pillar standing at the bottom of Wesley Slope in Christchurch Street West is there for? It was part of a grand design by Frome solicitor Thomas Bunn (1766–1853) to build a grand crescent, similar to those in Bath, and the pillar was one of four meant to mark the entrance roads from each end. Bunn described them as being of an 'elegant design and are intended to better the rest of the town which has hitherto delighted in deformity'. However, erecting the stone pillars was the furthest the scheme got.

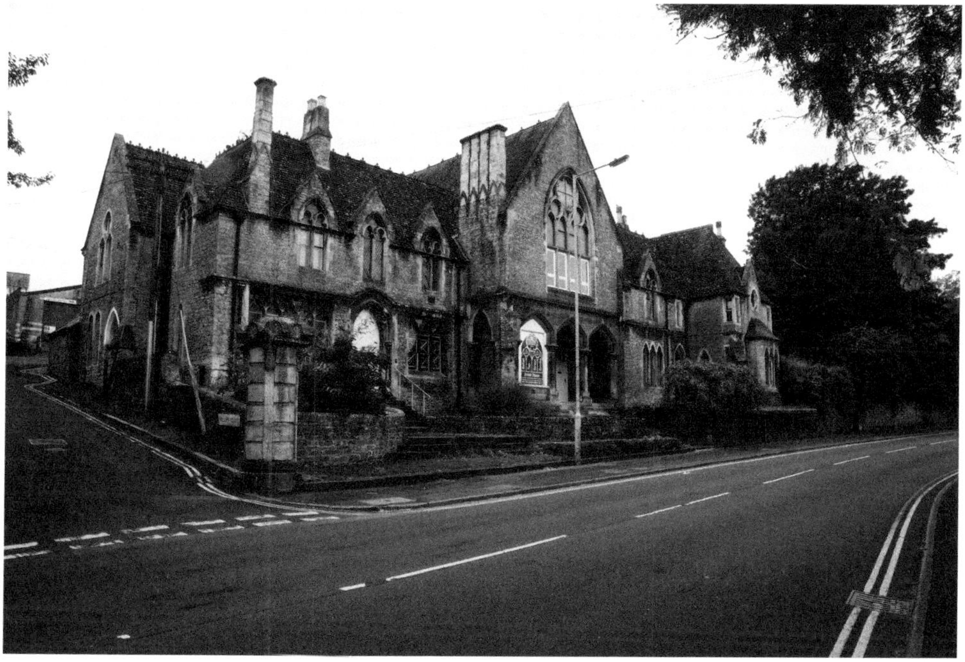

Old police station with Bunn's column in foreground. (Martin Kearley)

The Trinity area of Frome is recognised as an exceptionally early example of planned, as opposed to ad hoc urban development in modern times. From around the start of the eighteenth century it provided a multitude of new homes for a rapidly expanding proletarian community of workers in the manufacture of cloth. Agricultural improvements generated further wealth in the region in the eighteenth and nineteenth centuries. A ruined lean-to shelter style of limekiln in Vallis Vale is one of many that can be seen in fields around Frome. These structures, Somerset's most numerous type of historic industrial monument, provided lime for improving acidic soils and for mortar and other building materials.

Despite its importance as a cloth manufacturing centre and its proximity to the north Somerset coalfield, Frome was not connected to the canal network that was so significant in the industrialisation of its manufacturing neighbours, Trowbridge and Bradford-on-Avon, across the border in Wiltshire. A spur off the Kennet & Avon Canal, which would have served the town, was projected in a grand scheme to extend the navigation to the south coast. Work on this new 'Somerset & Dorset Canal' started in 1786 but, for financial reasons, it was abandoned in 1803. A substantial amount of work was accomplished in this time and there is plenty of evidence of the unfinished canal to be seen around Vobster and Mells. Two aqueducts were built – one at Murtry and another at Vallis Vale – both of which have survived.

Although the canal never reached Frome, the railway did. Its train shed, designed in Brunel's draughting office, is celebrated among railway history enthusiasts as the earliest surviving example in the country. Bath Street, a new road designed to accommodate the

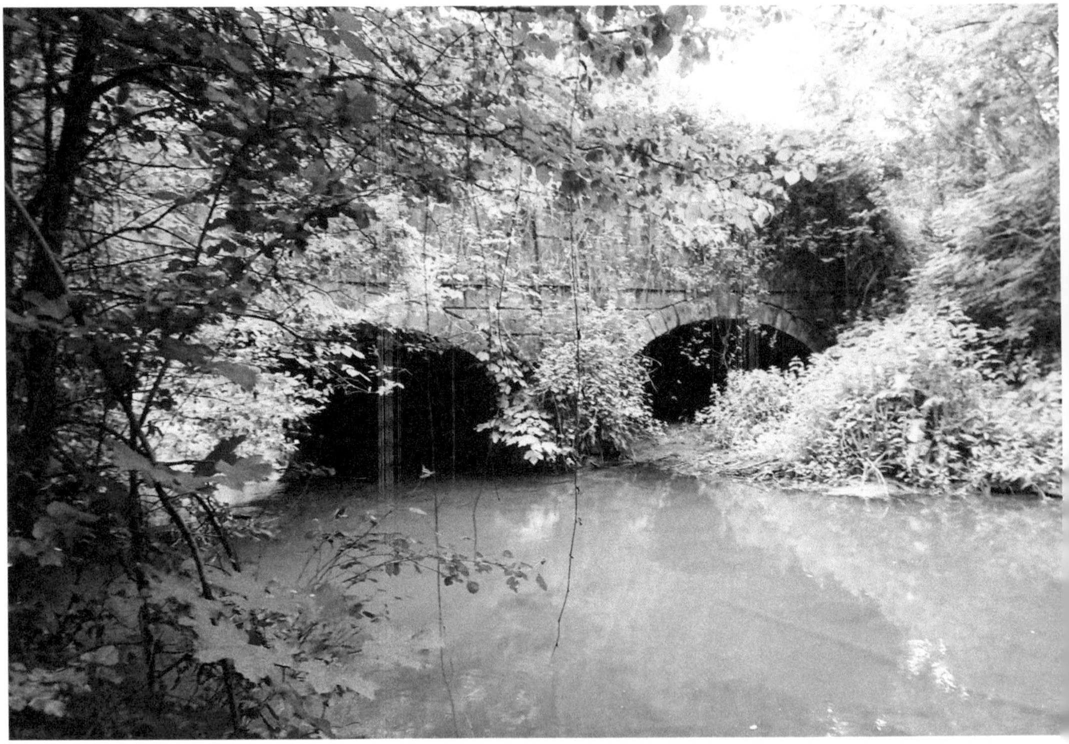

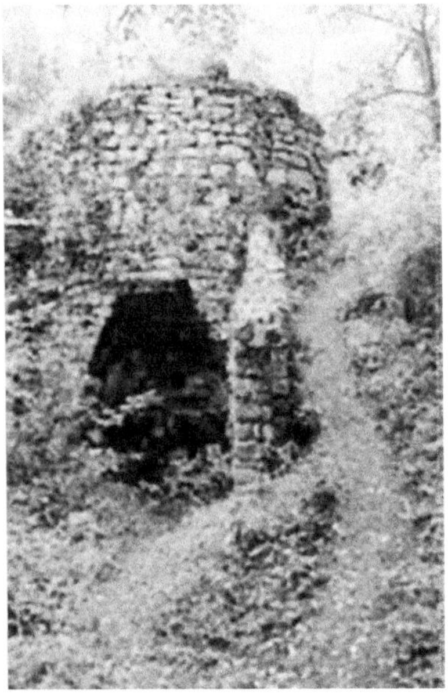

Above: Murtry Aqueduct, built to take the canal over Mells River. (Gary Kearley)

Left: Disused limekiln in picturesque Vallis Vale. (Gary Kearley)

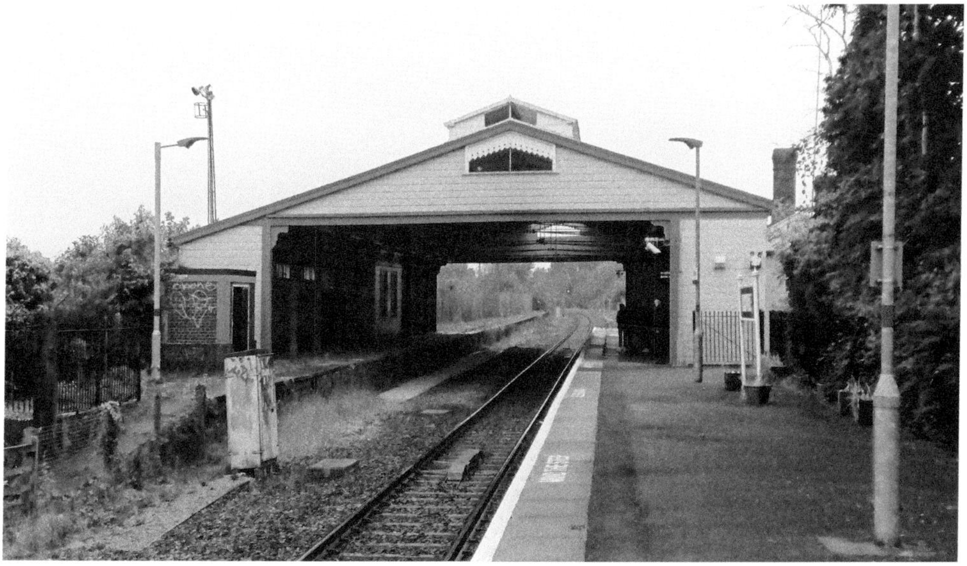

Above: Frome station's train shed. (Gary Kearley)

Right: Frome Heritage Museum. (Gary Kearley)

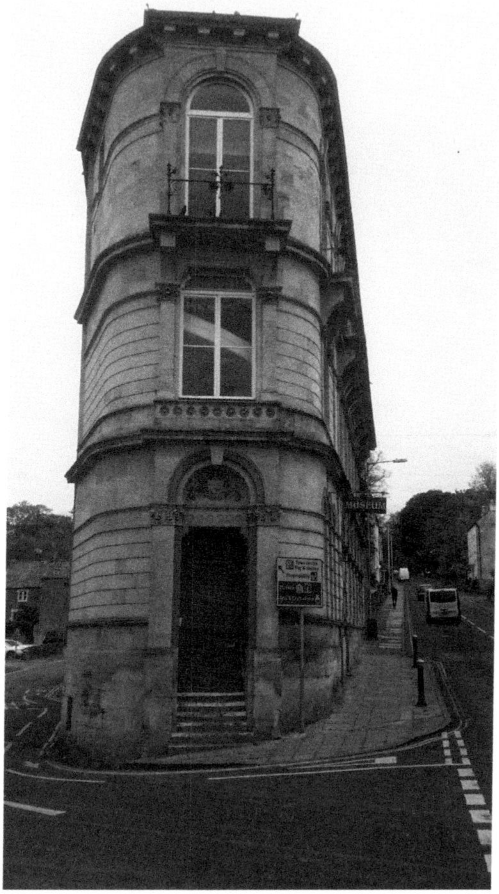

increasing amount of four-wheeled traffic heading in and out of the town centre, was cut early in the nineteenth century. Its name does not denote a route to Bath but instead celebrates Lord Weymouth of Longleat, who had been recently honoured with a new title as Marquess of Bath. New amenities in the Victorian 'age of improvement' included the establishment of the Literary and Scientific Institute in purpose-built premises constructed in 1868. This extraordinary building at the foot of North Parade, designed to look like the prow of an ocean liner, is now home to the Frome Heritage Museum. The new Victoria Hospital and public baths, the Victoria Baths, were built and named for the queen's diamond jubilee. New and improved schools, theatres and provisions for sports followed in the twentieth century.

The threat of invasion from France remained a constant worry throughout the eighteenth and nineteenth centuries and drill halls were established to train volunteers. Twattle Alley, which ran along the southern edge of the churchyard, was closed in around 1840 and a rifle range was built into the former roadway in 1860 by instruction of Captain James Wickham, who leased the adjoining house in Gentle Street. This served as the main training base for the local yeomanry up until 1914 when a new drill hall was opened on Keyford, behind the current fire station. The Keyford drill hall still fulfils a military role as a base for the Frome branch of the Somerset Army Cadets and, until recently, the Frome Air Cadets, whereas the one in Twattle Alley saw a number of uses including a skittle alley before being tastefully converted into a private house. The legend painted on the door commemorates its use by Prince Albert's Somersetshire Light Infantry, 3rd Volunteer Battalion, in 1889.

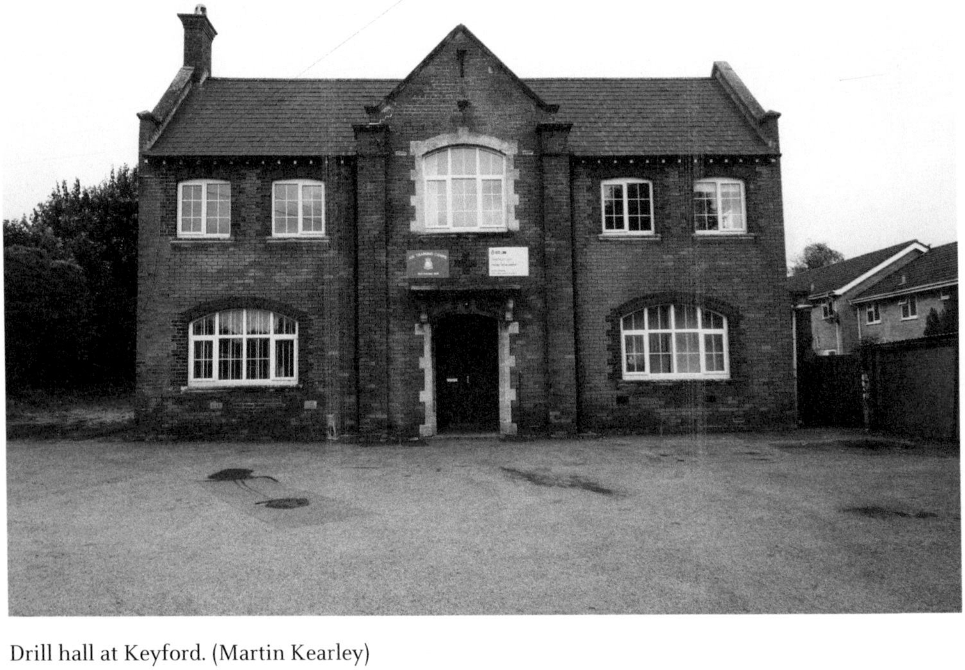

Drill hall at Keyford. (Martin Kearley)

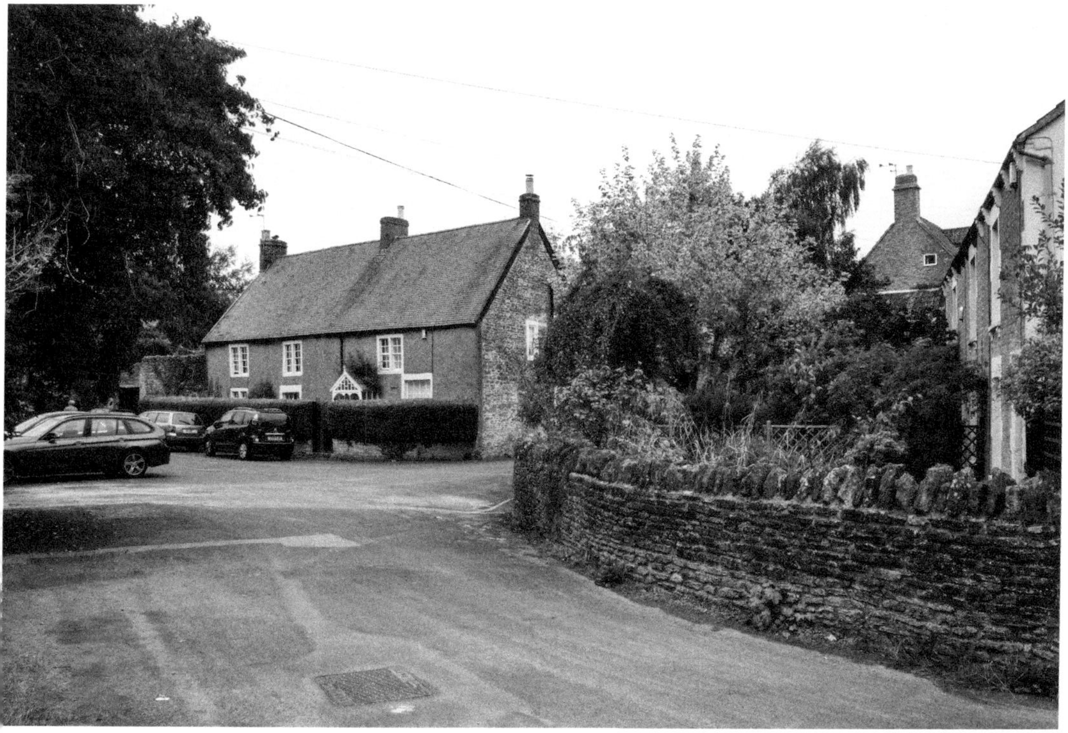

Keyford, once a separate hamlet, retains its village feel. (Martin Kearley)

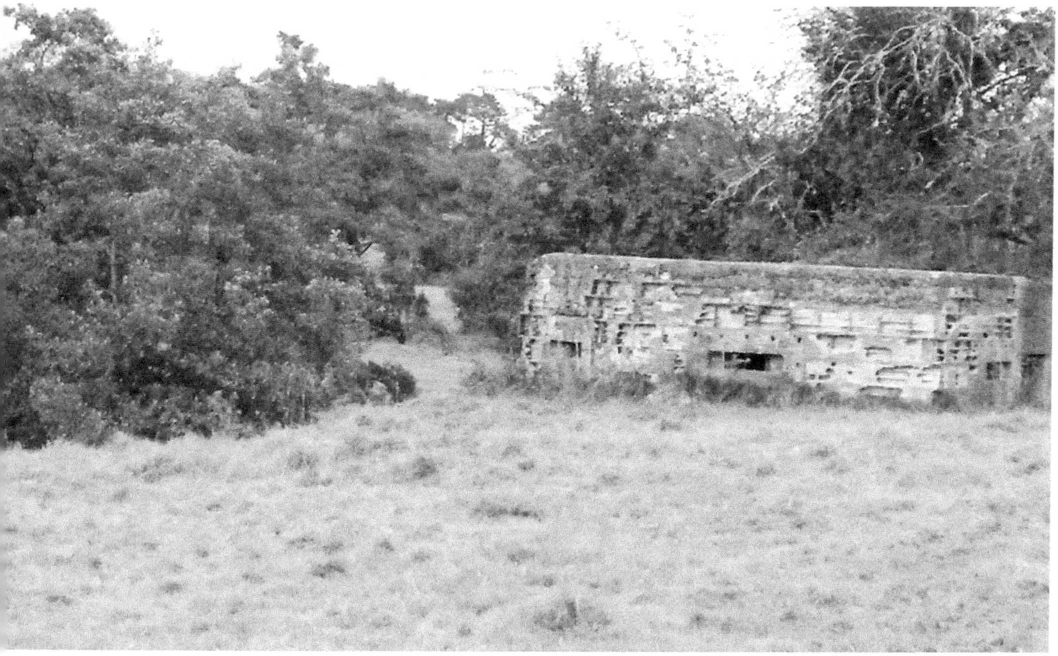

Pillbox near Shawford Bridge. (Gary Kearley)

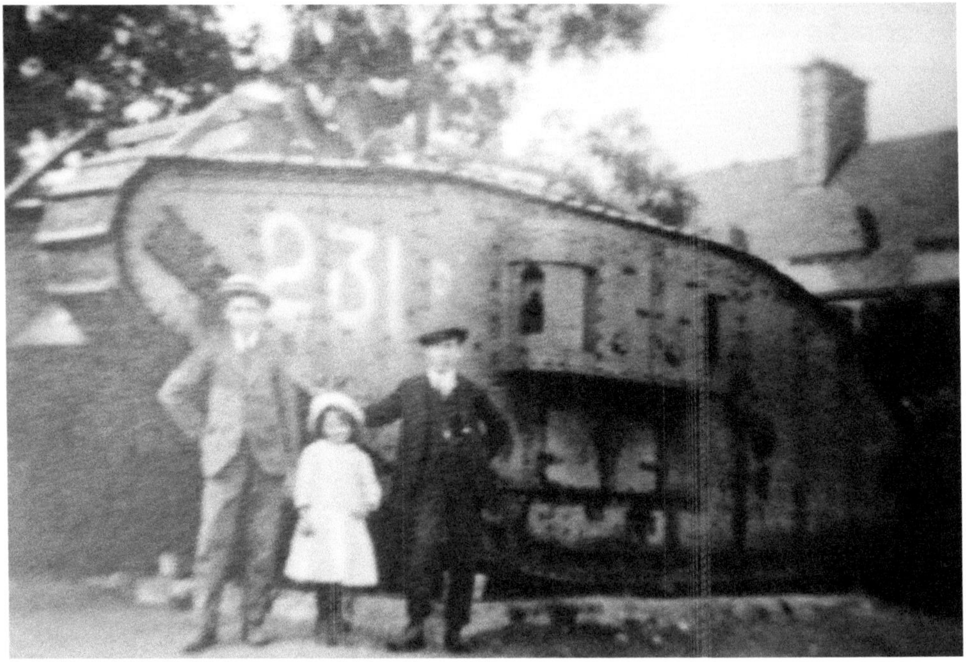

First World War tank in Frome's Recreation Grounds.

The General Headquarters (GHQ) line, which runs close to Frome, is a massive defensive construction designed to counter an invasion of Britain in the Second World War. It takes full advantage of the defensive value of rivers and canals in the region and elsewhere lengths of ditch were dug, 5 metres wide and 3 metres deep. Numerous pillbox gun emplacements and concrete block tank traps can be seen along its course. In addition to the GHQ line, the Ringwood West line and the Taunton stop line also stretched across Somerset.

Frome's war memorial stands outside the Memorial Theatre in Christchurch Street West. Older residents remember another, more unusual memorial, a First World War tank that for nearly twenty years sat in the Recreation Grounds. Frome residents had raised over half a million pounds for the war effort and their generosity was marked by the presentation of the tank. It duly arrived by rail in December 1919 and was driven through the streets to the 'Rec' by a Lt McNab. By 1938 the Mark IV 'female' tank No. 231, which had seen active service throughout the First World War, had become somewhat neglected and was becoming a bit of an eyesore, the *Somerset Standard* calling it an 'enrusted blot' on the area. The decision was made to sell it and it was eventually purchased in 1938 by G. Walter (Bath) Ltd, with the £22 10*s* raised (£22.50) being handed to the Royal British Legion. One wonders if it was recycled into a new tank in time for the outbreak of the Second World War the following year.

Think about car production in the UK and Longbridge, Cowley, Sunderland and Dagenham all come to mind, but back in the early 1900s Frome was also a centre of motor car production, albeit on a much smaller scale, with two rival manufacturers.

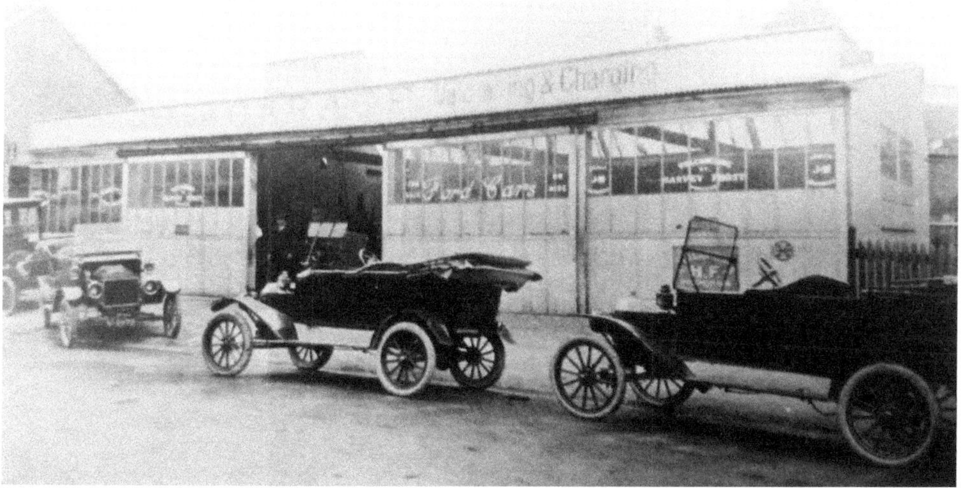

Above: Frome's car assembly plant.

Right: War memorial on Christchurch Street West. (Gary Kearley)

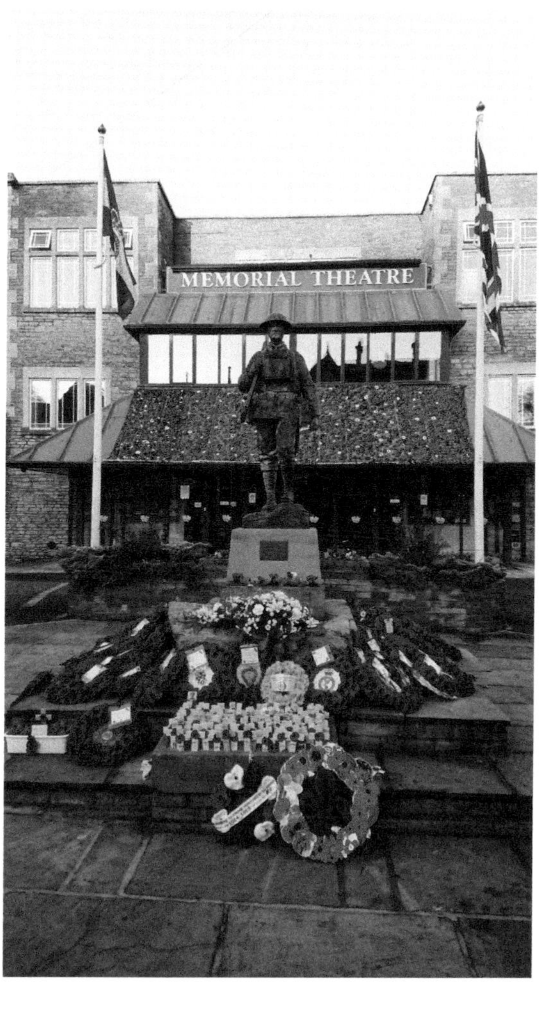

From around 1901 to 1908 (when the famous Model T Ford first went into production in America) B. Thompson Engineers Ltd (later Frome Selwood Motor Works) produced the Achilles from premises in Keyford and Butts Hill. An Achilles would set you back between £145 and £300 according to the level of finish. Eastmead and Biggs meanwhile were producing the Voiturette in their workshop in Christchurch Street East for the competitive price of £225.

Most of the major components were brought in for assembly in Frome, although some parts were locally produced and all of the coachwork was done in-house. Many of the cars made in Frome were purchased by locals, although Goodall's Automobile Agency was appointed to handle sales in London and the Home Counties. One interesting aside is that car owners had free rein to licence their new cars anywhere in the country and many chose remote Radnorshire in Wales, because they were loath to pay licence fees to local authorities who (like London for example) employed so-called anti-motoring police, who operated 'motor traps'. A tyre factory, Wallington, Weston & Co., was based in the premises of what became the Cuprinol paint factory. The old Eastmead and Biggs car assembly shop in Christchurch Street East is now home to a tyre and exhaust fitting company.

In Victorian England funicular railways were all the rage at popular seaside haunts such as Lynmouth, Hastings and Torbay, but as recently as the year 2000 plans were submitted for one to be built in Frome. The idea was to run a line 60 metres from Cork Street to the top of Catherine Hill in an attempt to attract more tourists to the town and to revitalise the top end of town, which was then in dire need of support. The venture

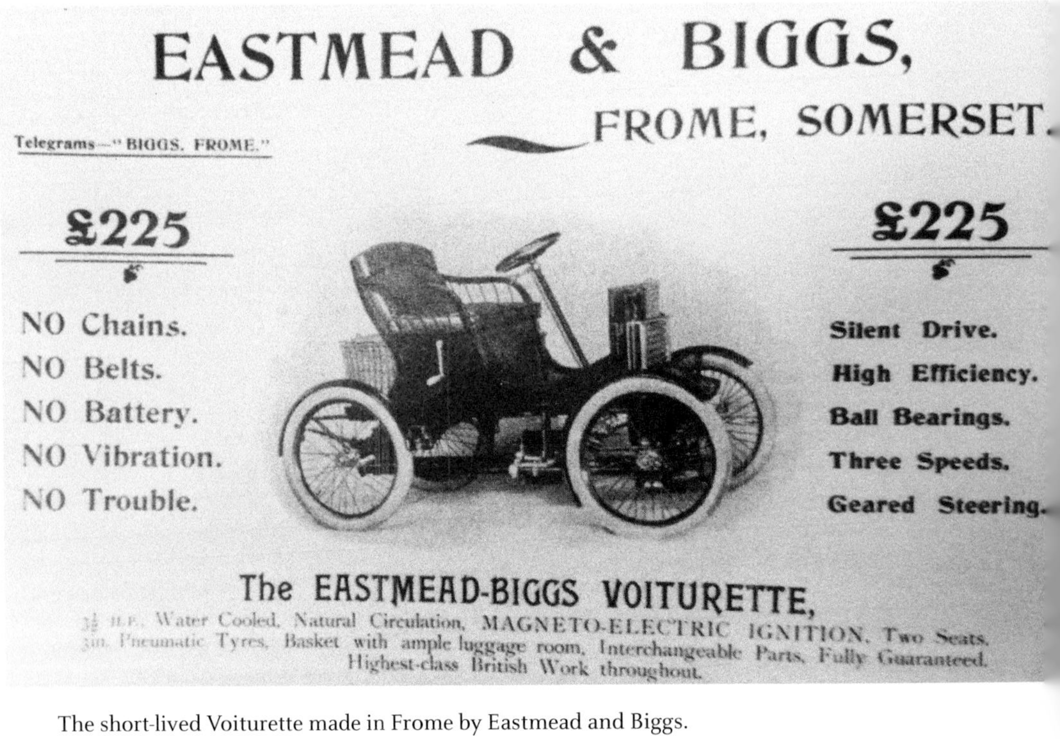

The short-lived Voiturette made in Frome by Eastmead and Biggs.

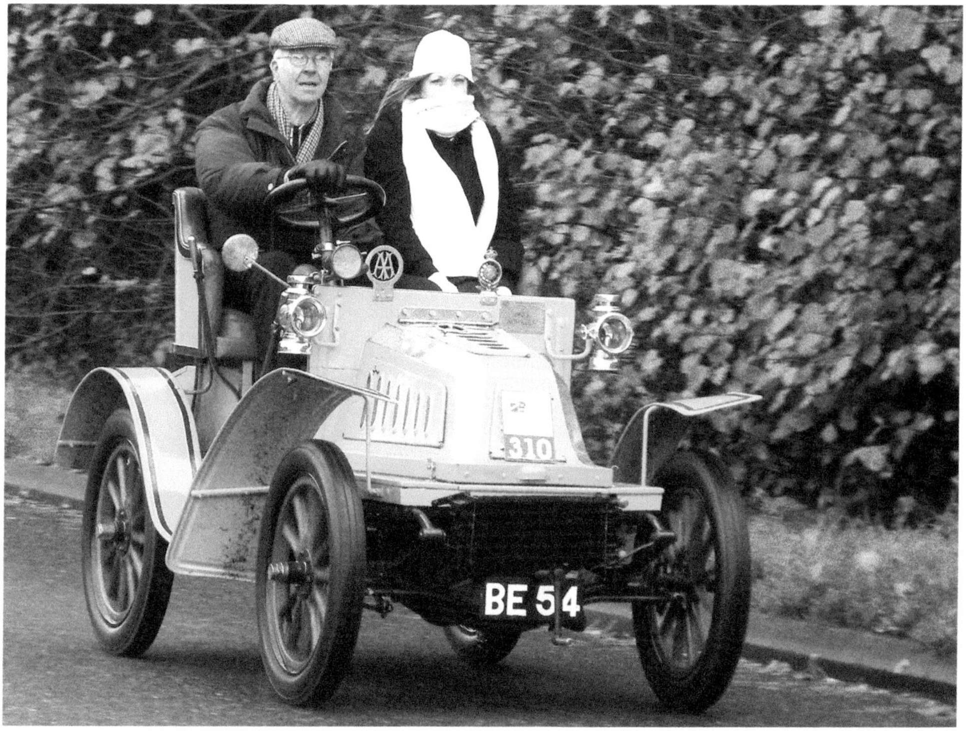

Frome-built Achilles, 2008 London to Brighton veteran car run.

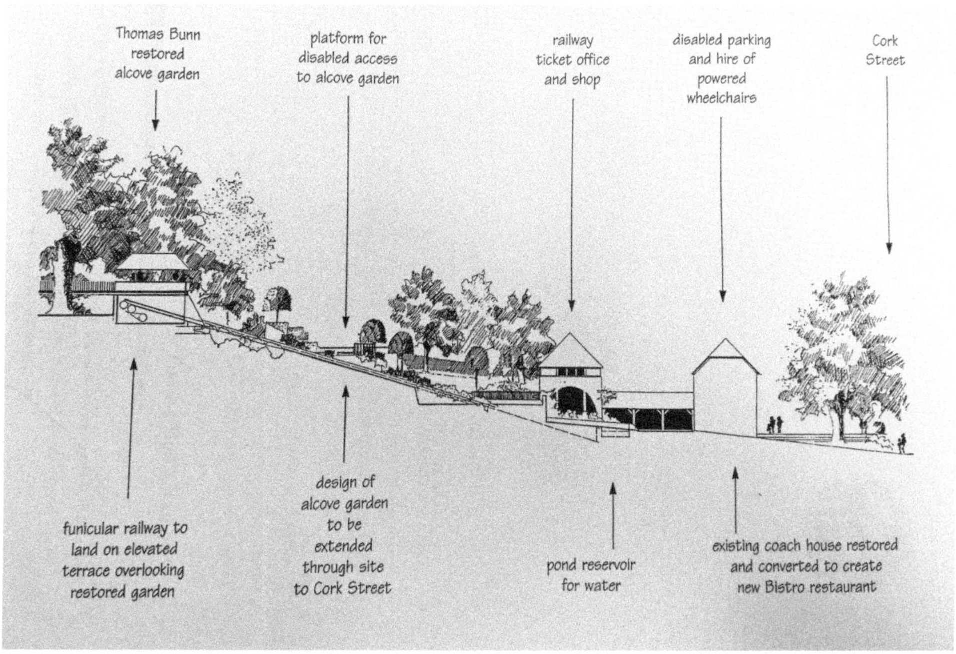

Plans for Frome's funicular railway.

was supported by the local MP, Frome Town Council, Mendip District Council and the local Chamber of Trade. It was to be called the Thomas Bunn Railway after the local lawyer who had been responsible for the cutting of Bath Street in the early 1800s and through whose former garden the railway was intended to run. The gardens were to be restored and new retail outlets, workshops, and a nursing home were planned as part of the regeneration. Funding for the £950,000 project was sought from the Millennium Commission and land was made available by the council at a discounted price. In the end the project came to nothing, although the nursing home was built amid unsubstantiated rumours that the whole business had been concocted purely to obtain the land for the nursing home cheaply.

Frome has always had a strong sense of community. The Community Fridge in Justice Lane was established by Edventure: Frome in partnership with Frome Town Council and is the first of its kind anywhere in the UK, where businesses or individuals can deposit unwanted food, which can then be taken free of charge by anyone in need. This has recently been supplemented by a Community Larder for non-chilled products.

DID YOU KNOW?
The former Selwood Hospital in Weymouth Road, now converted into housing (Ecos Court), was originally Frome's workhouse, built following the passing of the Poor Law Amendment Act of 1834. It was designed to house up to 350 inmates and built in a hexagonal form.

The Milk Street brewery and other microbreweries in the area have helped to resurrect an old Frome manufacturing tradition. When John Strachey wrote about the place in the mid-1730s, he declared Frome 'is famous for strong beer in October so that a little ale house as to outward appearance shall often have 100 hogsheads of excellent liquor'.

Used for so long and by so many people, sometimes the worse for drink, it is not surprising that Frome's pubs have an especially rich social history and that they have spawned plenty of local legends. Certainly they have had a reputation for being potentially dangerous places – places where drink-fuelled fights break out, sometimes with dreadful consequences. In 1774 the body of someone thought to have been killed by Joshua Yeomans, the landlord of the White Hart on Market Place, was found floating in the river nearby. At least two men were killed in pub brawls in Frome in 1820s: John Crees in 1823 in a fight that spilled out of the Blue Boar, Market Place, and a Mr Butcher, who got into a fight with four Irishmen in the Angel & Crown on Vallis Way in 1830. Eight years later poor Emma Hoddinott, wife of the landlord of the George at Marston Bigot, died of fright when her husband tried to break up a fight between customers. There is a grim history of Frome landlords killing themselves, intentionally or otherwise. In 1796 John Neal, landlord of the Swan at Badcox, died in a large beer cask, after being overcome by fumes when attempting to retrieve some dregs to make a poultice for one of

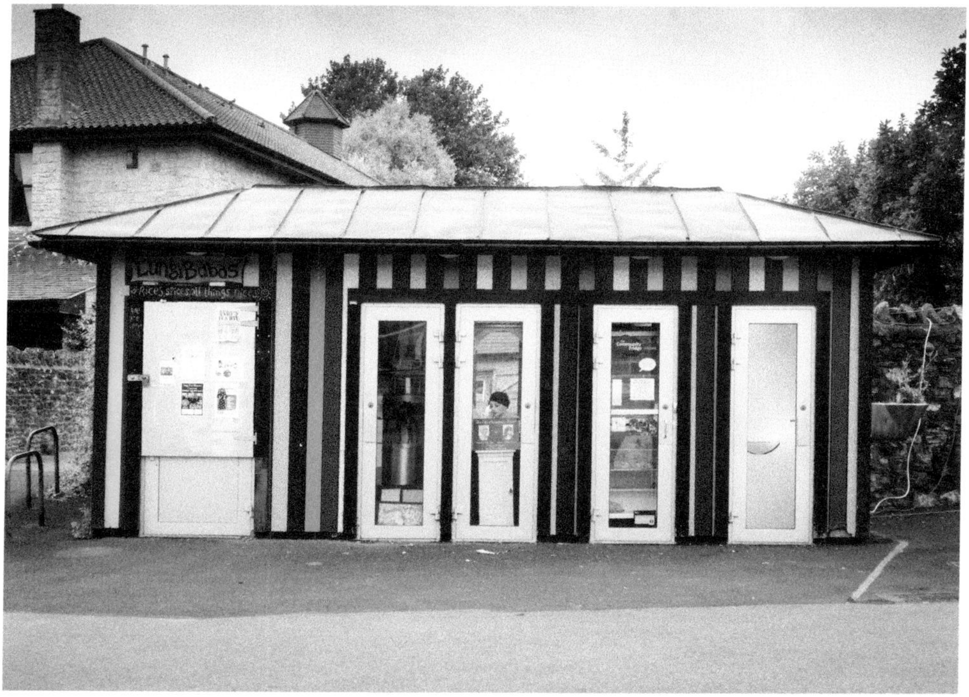

Community Fridge in Justice Lane, the first in the country. (Martin Kearley)

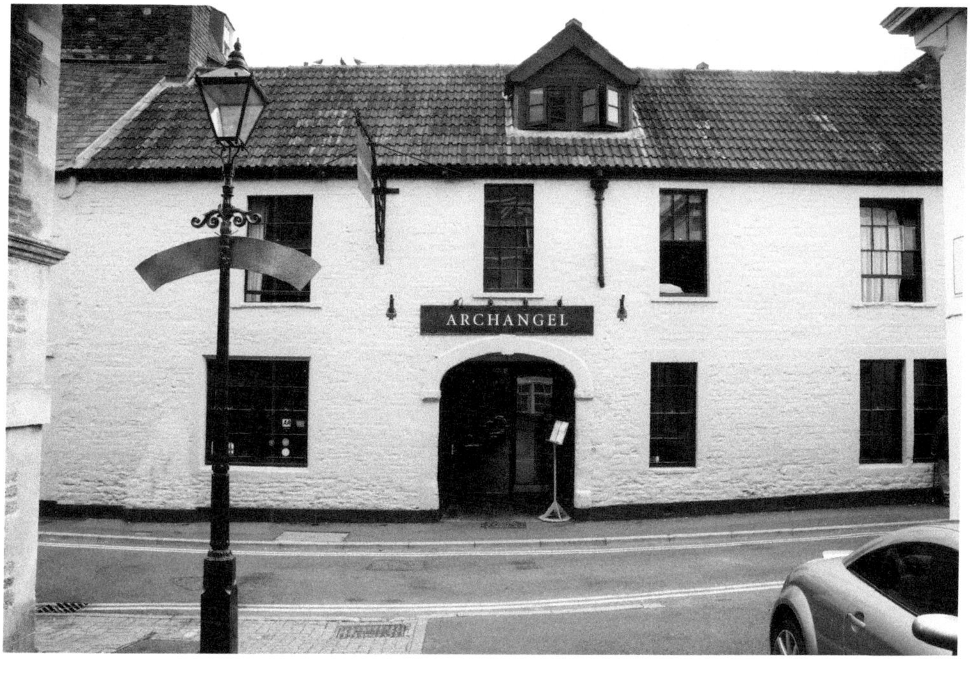

The Archangel, an inn since 1311. (Martin Kearley)

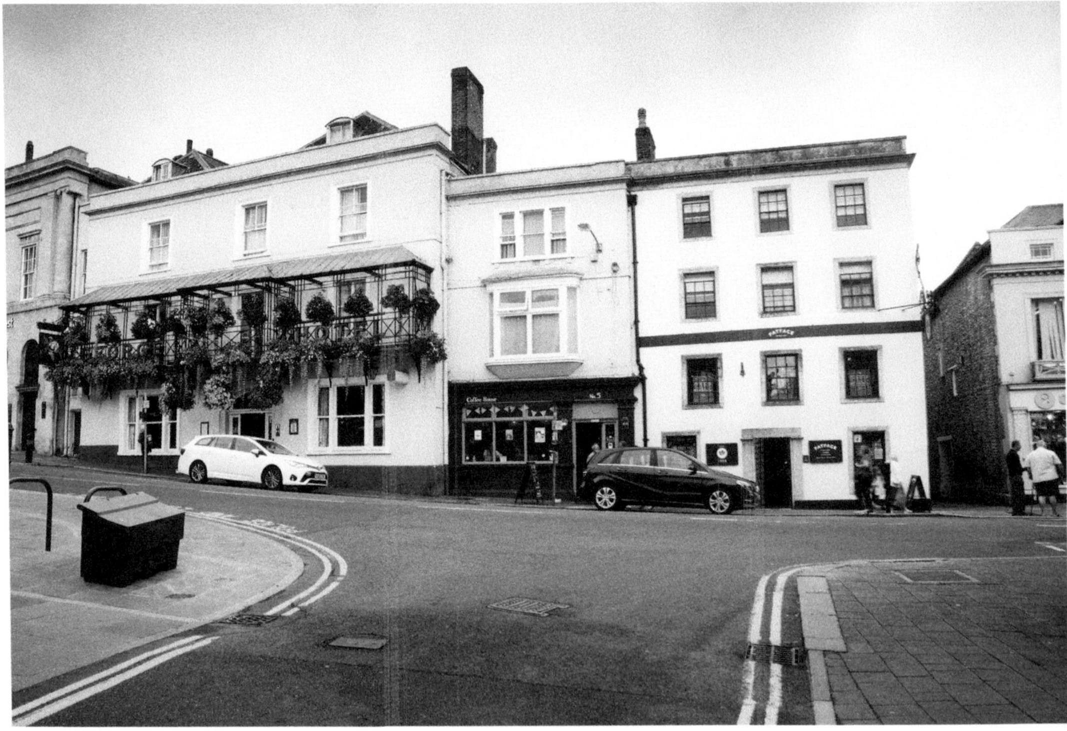

The Old Crown Inn, now Fatface. (Martin Kearley)

his children. Publican suicides include Henry Taylor, landlord of the Kings Head, Trinity Street, who, in 1838, shot himself in the pub's outside privy. In 1887 Benjamin Gunning, landlord of the Sun, Catherine Street, died after throwing himself out of his bedroom window, and in 1946 Sebright Jones, landlord of the Beehive, Keyford, fell down the stairs and fractured his skull. Frome made national news in 1931 when sixty-seven-year-old Sir William Bull, a baronet and former Conservative MP for Hammersmith, dropped down dead when giving a speech in the George.

Such gloomy occurrences in their history perhaps explain the preponderance of the pub-poltergeist. Unexplained activity has been recorded in the Griffin, the Wheatsheaves and the Lamb and Fountain, among others. On one occasion at the Griffin in Milk Street a woman ordered a drink that came in a tall wine glass. Before she could pay, the glass flew off the end of the bar leaving just the stem behind. The barman said that it was as if someone had hit the glass with a hockey stick. The customer said nothing but left hastily! Customers who bring their dogs with them to the Griffin have reported that without warning all the dogs will go very still and stare at one of the walls, moving their heads in unison along the wall as if following something invisible to humans.

The Wheatsheaves on Bath Street has been exorcised on at least two occasions in order to get rid of the sound of a piano playing in the early hours. When asked why he didn't simply get rid of the piano, the then landlord replied, 'Because we haven't actually got a piano!'. On another occasion the landlord recalls a scruffy man approaching the bar and warning him. 'They are coming for you!'. Choosing to ignore the curious remark he asked the man what he wanted to drink. He ordered a bottle of Newcastle Brown from the shelf behind the bar but when the landlord turned back to his customer he had disappeared. Thinking that he had popped out to the toilet the landlord waited for him to return, but after five minutes there was still no sign of him. The other customers had not noticed him so, with a shrug, the drink was poured away. This episode, however, continued to bother the landlord, and he decided to pop up to the office and look at the CCTV footage. He was alarmed to see himself standing at the bar alone, talking to himself and turning around to fetch the bottle of beer for a non-existent customer! The poltergeist activity at the Lamb and Fountain has been rather low key, limited it seems to bottles falling off shelves in the middle of the night. Some regulars reckon they can account for the mystery: it really is a very ancient pub, thought to date back to the 1520s, and its walls, floors and shelves are not as level as they might have been when first built.

On 13 October 1961 (fittingly Friday the thirteenth) *The Western Gazette* reported a tunnel discovered below the Old Bell Studios on Catherine Street. The new owners had begun to feel 'uneasy' when visiting their cellars and this 'unpleasant atmosphere' was also felt by a visitor from Canvey Island who, professing to have some powers in such matters, claimed to be able to see a cavity under the cellar floors, with running water, the level of which could be raised or lowered to drown people imprisoned there. She also claimed that she could see 'dismembered bones and lime and dark-skinned people'. Fearing that the cellars might be haunted, the owner arranged for the floor to be lifted and discovered that there was indeed a tunnel, 18 inches wide and around 4 feet high, with running water, going under all three of the cellars. A blockage after 75 yards in one direction and a sharp bend in the other direction prevented further investigation so the other claims remain unproven. Were the bones from an unconsecrated burial ground further up the hill or something more sinister, or, indeed, mere fantasy? The article ends with a letter from Mr. O. C. Sigurdson, who said that he had lived in the property with his family for five years with no problems of any kind. The reference to 'dark-skinned people' is curious but ties in with reports from one resident of High Street whose property has gravestones in the cellar; it is said that on occasion he would wake in the middle of the night to find the apparition of a black man sitting on the end of his bed. The two properties are less than a hundred metres apart.

Answering a knock on their door one day, residents of a house on Willow Vale found an old gentleman who said that he used to live there and, as he was passing, thought he would call in. He told them several tales about his time there and then asked them if they had found the horse yet. In response to their perplexed expressions, he went on to tell them of the old practice of the local farmers who used to leave their horses and carts in Willow Vale while they adjourned to the pub on market days. On one occasion they returned to find that his father's horse had passed away, still strapped into its harness. Not knowing quite what to do they called on the 'strong man' of Frome, who happened to live nearby, and with his help they were able to deposit the departed nag in a large hole dug in their garden. In it went, on its back, the man related, with its four stiff legs sticking up before being buried. The householders smiled politely and dismissed the old chap's story until one day, while doing some gardening, they came across a horseshoe, hoof still attached, sticking out of the ground! Soon the skeletal remains of a further three equine legs were unearthed nearby. The greatest secrets, it is said, are always hidden in the most unlikely places.

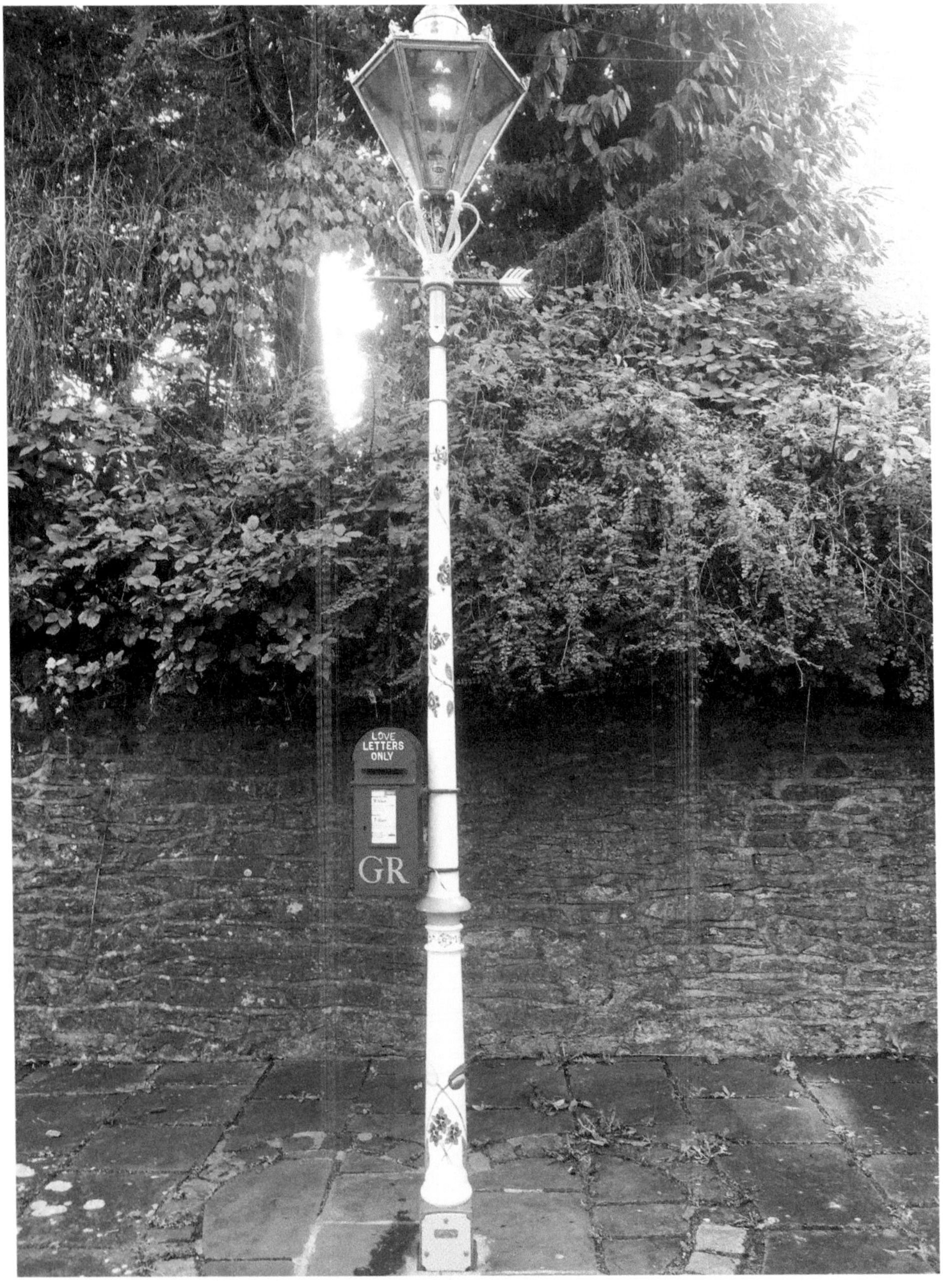

The Valentine Lamp, the last working gaslight in Somerset. (Andrew Pickering)

Sources

Anon., *Great News from the West of England* (London: 1689)
Anon., *The North Somerset Yeomanry Cavalry* (Bath: H. E. Carringtons, 1850)
Anon., *Frome St John the Baptist Church Guide* (Frome: The Parish of Frome St John the Baptist, undated)
Anon., *Frome, Somerset: The Official Guide* (Frome: Frome Town Council, undated)
Athill, Robin, *Old Mendip* (Frome: Bran's Head, 1984)
Barratt, John, *Battlefield Britain: The Civil War in the South-West* (Barnsley: Pen and Sword, 2005)
Barrett, J. H., 'Tom Tivey's Hole rock shelter, near Leighton, Somerset',*Proceedings of the University of Bristol Spelaeological Society*, 11:1 (1966), 9–24
Barry, Jonathan, *Witchcraft and Demonology in South-West England, 1640–1789.* (London: Palgrave Macmillan, 2012)
Bates, E. H., (ed.), *Quarter Sessions Records of the County of Somerset, 1625–1639* (Taunton: Somerset Record Society,1908)
Baxter, Richard, *The Certainty of the Worlds of Spirits.* (London: 1691)
Belham, Peter, *The Making of Frome* (Frome: Frome Society for Local Study, 1985)
Bernard, Richard, *A Guide to Grand-Jury Men [...] in cases of witchcraft, etc.* (London: 1627)
Bird, Sheila, *The Book of Somerset Villages* (Wimborne: The Dovecote Press, 1986)
Body, Geoffrey, *The A–Z of Curious Somerset* (Stroud: The History Press, 2013)
Bush, Robin, *Somerset Bedside Book* (Wimborne: The Dovecote Press, 1997)
Byford, Enid, *Somerset Curiosities* (Wimborne: The Dovecote Press, 1987)
—. *Somerset Murders* (Wimborne: The Dovecote Press, 1990)
Cleverdon, F. W., *A History of Mells* (Frome: Frome Society for Local History, 1974)
Cuzner, Stephen, *Hand-book to Frome-Selwood* (Frome: 1866)
Dunning, Robert (ed.), *Christianity in Somerset* (Taunton: Somerset County Council, 1975)
Gill, Derek J., *Frome* (Stroud: Alan Sutton, 1995)
Glanvill, Joseph, *Saducismus Triumphatus, or, full and plain Evidence concerning Witches and Apparitions* (London: 1681)
Hawkins, Mac, *Somerset at War* (Wimborne: Dovecote Press, 1996)
Jefferson, Joyce (ed.), *The Book of Leigh Upon Mendip* (Westbury: Leigh History Group, 2010)
Goodall, Rodney, *The Buildings of Frome* (Frome: Frome Society for Local Study, 2013)
MacLeay, Alastair, (ed.), *Frome Society Year Book, volumes 14 & 18* (Frome: Frome Society for Local Study, 2011, 2015)
McGarvie, Michael, *The Bounds of Selwood.* (Frome: Frome Society for Local Study, 1978)
—. *The Book of Frome: A History* (Buckingham: Barracuda Books, 1980)

—. *Frome Place Names: Their Origin and Meaning* (Frome: Frome Society for Local Study, 1983)
—. *Crime and Punishment in Regency Frome: The Journals of Isaac Gregory, Constable of Frome 1813–14 and 1817–18* (Frome: Frome Society for Local Study, 1984)
—. *Frome Through the Ages* (Frome: Frome Society for Local Study, 2000)
Palmer, Kingsley, *The Folklore of Somerset* (London: Batsford, 1976)
Pickering, Andrew, *The Witches of Selwood Forest: Witchcraft and Demonism in the West of England, 1625–1700.* (Newcastle upon Tyne: Cambridge Scholars Publishing, 2017)
—. 'Witchcraft and evidence in a Somerset parish in the seventeenth century', *The Local Historian*, 48: 1 (2018), 30–40
—. 'Great News from the West of England: Witchcraft and Strange Vomiting in a Somerset Village', *Magic, Ritual and Witchcraft*, 13: 1 (2018), 71–97
Rose-Troup, Frances, *The Western Rebellion of 1549* (London: Smith Elder & Co., 1931)
Sly, Nicola, *A Grim Almanac of Somerset* (Stroud: The History Press, 2010)
Summerscale, Kate, *The Suspicions of Mr Wicher* (London: Bloomsbury, 2008)
Sweet, Jack, *Shocking Somerset Stories* (Tiverton: Somerset Books, 1999)
Thornes, Robin, *Men of Iron: The Fussells of Mells* (Frome: Frome Society for Local Study, 2010)
Tongue, Ruth, *Somerset Folklore* (Glasgow: The Folklore Society, 1965)
Underdown, David, *Somerset in the Civil War and Interregnum* (Newton Abbot: David & Charles, 1973)
—. *Revel, Riot, and Rebellion: Popular Politics and Culture in England, 1603–1660.* (Oxford: Oxford University Press, 1985)
Webster, C., Mayberry, M, *The Archaeology of Somerset* (Wellington: Somerset Books, 2007)
Wigfield, W, Macdonald, *The Monmouth Rebels: 1685* (Taunton: Somerset Record Society, 1985)
Somerset Historic Environment Record.

Acknowledgements

The authors have been greatly assisted in their enquiries by the Frome Tunnels Project, staff at Frome Heritage Museum, members of the Frome Society for Local Study, and the librarians and archivists at the Somerset Heritage Centre. They also extend their thanks to Martin Kearley and Robin Rowland Hill for providing many of the contemporary photographs. Except where noted or where the provenance is unknown, all images are deemed to be licensed under the Creative Commons Attribution-Share Alike 3.0 Unported license: https://creativecommons.org/licenses/by-sa/3.0/deed.en.

About the Authors

Andrew Pickering is Programme Manager for a University of Plymouth degree delivered at Strode College in Street, Somerset. He has written several books and papers on the history of witchcraft beliefs in Selwood Forest and elsewhere. He has delivered numerous talks on this and other subjects in and around Frome, where he lived for several years before moving to his present home in Bruton. His most recent publication, *Steinbeck and the Matter of Arthur,* is an account of the time John Steinbeck lived in the vicinity while he was researching the legends of King Arthur and his Knights of the Round Table.

Gary Kearley has a first class honours degree in History, Heritage and Archaeology. He is a volunteer at Frome Heritage Museum and an expert in the history and archaeology of Frome's elusive tunnels, frequently leading tours and giving presentations on the discoveries of the Frome Tunnels Project. Gary has lived in Frome for twenty years.